MASCULINE POWER,
FEMININE BEAUTY

Masculine Power, Feminine Beauty

The Volitional, Objective Basis for Heterosexuality in Romantic Love and Marriage

Ronald Pisaturo

with additional essays by
Charlotte Cushman
and Jeffrey Perren

Second Edition
Revised October 8, 2023

ISBN 978-0-9997041-7-2 (Paperback)

Contents

PREFACE

The first edition of this book began as a series of blog posts, each installment of which I published before writing the next. In editing those blog posts into a book, I reorganized some content and improved formulations throughout. Since the publication of the first edition, I have written several articles and blog posts that improved upon the formulations in the book. Moreover, I have made further identifications, especially regarding heterosexuality in romantic love (Chapter 1). I am pleased to be able to include this improved and new content in a second edition.

This new edition also includes essays (Appendices 4 and 5) from two other authors, whom I asked to write some of their own thoughts on masculinity and femininity. These essays illustrate that rational ideas on these subjects can vary while remaining within an objective range. These authors do not necessarily agree with everything I have written in the book, and vice versa. But I do think that what they have written is very much worth reading.

This book offers an objective alternative to the following false alternative regarding the subject of sexual orientation: the authority of religion vs. the subjectivism that has infected much of modern philosophy, science, and culture. (That is not to say that the book is as critical of the contemporary Christian conception of sexual orientation as it is of the contemporary "LGBT" conception.) The book also offers an account of the differences between men and women that recognizes the utmost intellectual ability, rationality, and resultant moral virtue possible in equal measure to each sex.

Since the first edition in 2015, the influence of postmodernism and so-called "critical theory" has reached pandemic proportions, in the form of "critical race theory," "intersectionality," "gender studies," "social justice," "cancel culture," "wokeness," and the like. My treatment of the LGBT movement in Chapters 3 through 5, edited only lightly from the first edition, shows that all of the main philosophical elements of the present cultural pandemic were already present in the LGBT movement. Indeed, the LGBT movement was an early outbreak, into the general public, of the present pandemic.

This book is on philosophy, not psychology. In my judgment, the subject of romantic love is the unidentified sixth branch of philosophy, on a par with esthetics. It is no accident that most major Western philosophers in history have written about love.

Just as a response to a work of art is a sympathetic response to what Ayn Rand ([1966] 1975, 28) calls "metaphysical value-judgments" implicit in the art work, so a romantic response is a sympathetic response to metaphysical value-judgments implicit in the person loved. In Chapter 2, I discuss parallels between love and art, relying heavily on writings of Ayn Rand.

In the book, I analyze numerous writings in the field of psychology, but I do so in order to identify philosophic premises and philosophic errors.

I do travel to the borderline of philosophy and psychology in at least two important and related respects: one, regarding the nature of free will; and two, regarding the relation between reason and emotion. I hope that some readers will find my philosophical thoughts useful when crossing the border from philosophy into psychology. I for one am eager to learn what rational psychological inquiry can yet discover about sexual orientation.

The thinker to whom I am most indebted in all my writing, including this book, is Ayn Rand. (Of course, the judgments I express are the responsibility of me alone.) I quote extensively from Ayn Rand regarding the principle that emotional responses are based on chosen values.

The style that I use for citations is a version of the author-date system recommended by the *Chicago Manual of Style, 14th Edition*.

In this style, each source is cited briefly in the text by the author's last name (except that I use the full name "Ayn Rand," because it is a pen name), date of publication, and (where applicable) page numbers. The reader can use this brief citation to look up the source's full bibliographic information in the References section at the back of the book, just before the Index. The citation "Ayn Rand ([1966] 1975, 28)," on the previous page, refers to page 28 of a work by Ayn Rand, published in 1975; this publication is a reprint of a work published in 1966. The list of references at the back of the book identifies this work as "Philosophy and Sense of Life," reprinted in *The Romantic Manifesto*.

* * *

I would like to thank Glenn Marcus and Brad Thompson for their valuable comments on earlier drafts of the first edition of this book, and numerous discussions on the subject of the book. Brad convinced me that the rights related to children are a much more important legal aspect of marriage than I had realized.

Charlotte Cushman offered helpful suggestions to the second edition, and she improved my understanding of the feminine perspective on safety and intimacy.

All three of these individuals have very high standards for clarity, and they repeatedly encouraged me and pressed me to meet those standards throughout the book. Of course, the judgments expressed in this book, and any errors in it, are my own.

INTRODUCTION

> She knew, even though she was too young to know the
> reason, that indiscriminate desire and unselective in-
> dulgence were possible only to those who regarded sex
> and themselves as evil.
> —Ayn Rand, *Atlas Shrugged* (1957, 109 [Part 1, Chap-
> ter 5]).

> A sexual relationship is proper only on the ground of
> the highest values one can find in a human being. Sex
> must not be anything other than a response to values.
> And that is why I consider promiscuity immoral. Not
> because sex is immoral, but because sex is too good and
> too important.
> —Ayn Rand ([1964] n.d., 8).

This book is for individuals who know that romantic love, like
Romantic art, requires utmost selectivity. As Romanticism is a theory of art that entails such selectivity based on one's deepest values,
so I use the word "Romanticism" to denote an analogous theory of
romantic love.

For romantic love—as opposed to mindless, indiscriminate sexual contact—an individual must select, out of the whole world, only
one other person as his sexual partner. Given all the possible criteria
for selecting a partner, one must know which criteria are essential
and which are not, which are indeed consistent with one's deepest
values.

Is sex—or what is now called "gender," that is, whether one's sex
is male or female—one of these essential criteria, along with fundamental character traits such as honesty and integrity? Is it essential

for a man to select a woman and not another man? Or is sex a non-essential quality, such as hair color?

Individuals who are exclusively heterosexual or exclusively homosexual act in accordance with the premise that sex is indeed an essential criterion in selecting a romantic partner. Bisexuals may act as though sex is not essential.

For heterosexuals and homosexuals, what is the basis in each case for limiting the selection to one sex? Are the basis for heterosexuality and the basis for homosexuality equally rational, equally conducive to survival and happiness? Is "heterosexism"—the idea that heterosexuality is *better* than homosexuality, bisexuality, or other "sexual orientations"—an aspect of Romanticism, or is it like racism?

Moreover, does an individual even have a choice in whether he is romantically—which includes sexually—attracted to those of one sex or the other? If volition is involved, in what way is it involved in these attractions? Or are differences in sexual orientation determined by biological and environmental factors?

This book presents a theory of heterosexual romantic love. I argue that heterosexuality in particular enables romantic love in a way that integrates with all aspects of a man and woman. I argue also that sexual orientation is the result of volition in the same way that other aspects of romantic love are volitional. I discuss implications of my theory for the judging of homosexuality, and I debunk the mainstream theories that "affirm" non-heterosexual orientations. I then argue that objective cognition requires that the concept of marriage refer only to relationships between one man and one woman.

But an overarching theme of the book is that every individual should understand the reasons—specifically, the personal values—underlying his own sexual orientation.

My original motivation for studying this subject was to understand the differences between heterosexuality and other sexual orientations. But that initial motivation gave way to a much deeper one: to understand sexual orientation—or what I call "sex-specific sexual evaluation"—as a conceptually explicit, conscious conviction integrated with one's deepest values and emotions, instead of as a vague idea merely led by emotions.

Ayn Rand ([1966] 1975, 33) writes,

> Love is *the expression of philosophy*—of a subconscious philosophical sum—and, perhaps, no other aspect of human existence needs the *conscious* power of philosophy quite so desperately. When that power is called upon to verify and support an emotional appraisal, when love is a conscious integration of reason and emotion, of mind and values, then—and only then—it is the greatest reward of man's life.

I often use the terms "sex-specific sexual evaluation" or "sex-specific sexual values" instead of "sexual orientation" in order to emphasize that valuing one sex over another when it comes to sexual relations is a matter of values, not merely a matter of circumstances. I will use these three terms interchangeably.

In this book, I seek to demonstrate that an individual's sex-specific sexual evaluation is an integral part of the expression of his philosophy. By understanding his sex-specific sexual evaluation and what that evaluation implies for his relationship with his romantic partner, a man (or woman) can learn to express his identity more consistently, more thoroughly, and more joyfully.

Consistent with my theme, I argue that a terrible injustice has been committed against all individuals—heterosexual, homosexual, etc.—by the intellectual mainstream of the psychological and related professions, which have assured all individuals that there is no need to understand the source of their sexual orientation. I refute the schools of thought, now predominant to the point of virtual unanimity, that claim that sexual orientation is either the non-volitional product of heredity and/or society, or not even an objective concept.

Based on my theory of heterosexual romantic love, I do not see how there can be a comparably integrated theory of same-sex romantic love; but I invite anyone to present or reference such a theory.

This book takes radical stands—that is, fundamental, uncompromising stands that address the root of the issue—regarding philosophy, sexuality, and politics, three subjects famous for igniting passionate debate, praise, or condemnation. In criticizing homosexuality, some of the language I use is stern—but not gratuitous. At stake is not merely the well-being of adults, but of children taught by adults.

Nevertheless, to detractors and supporters alike, I offer—in good will—this challenge: I can explain how my sexual orientation is consistent with my other basic values; can you do the same for yours?

No other individual owes me an explanation of his sexual evaluations. But he owes such an explanation to himself.

In this book, I have chosen to explain my sex-specific sexual evaluations publicly, in the hope that doing so might help others understand their own and perhaps shed further light on this important subject.

> Man is born with certain physical and psychological
> needs, but he can neither discover them nor satisfy
> them without the use of his mind. Man has to discover
> what is right or wrong for him as a rational being. His
> so-called urges will not tell him what to do. —Ayn
> Rand ([1964] n.d., 9).

1. HETEROSEXUALITY IN ROMANTIC LOVE

In researching this book, I read numerous other accounts of the role of sex/gender in romantic love. Reading these other accounts convinced me that I had to write my own.

The theory I present in this chapter is based on my introspection, personal observations of myself and others, and contemplation of heroes and heroines in Romantic fiction. I am not seeking to describe an average or typical romantic relationship. I am seeking to describe a good one, one that may be rare, but one that is possible for anyone.

In Appendices 4 and 5, at my invitation, other individuals present their own thoughts on the role of sex/gender in romantic love. These appendices, in combination with the present chapter written by me, illustrate that no two senses of romance are exactly the same, but that they do fall within an understandable range.

As a statement of universal principles of heterosexual romantic love, the theory I present here is a hypothesis. As a statement of the reasons for my own heterosexuality, the theory is conviction.

In my exposition, I am deliberately omitting any advanced science to support my theory. The evidence for my theory is available to anyone—even a child—who has lived in Western civilization and had an opportunity to observe adult men and women. The evidence for my theory should have been available to Romeo, so that he could have understood why he was sexually attracted to Juliet and not Mercutio; and to Cyrano, so that he could have known why he was sexually attracted to Roxane and not Christian.

The thesis of this chapter has four factors:

1. Men have an inherited physical advantage over women: physical power.

2. It is rational for an individual to choose to capitalize on this physical advantage in his productive work and physical development.

3. Women have an inherited physical advantage over men: beauty as an end in itself.

4. A heterosexual relationship is a further, profound way to capitalize on the physical advantages of each sex.

I will discuss these four factors in order.

The body of a man and the body of a woman are similar, of course; each is a human body. Each has hands for manipulation, legs for locomotion, etc. Above all, each is guided by a reasoning mind. The primary use of anyone's body is in the activity of productive work (which can include raising children, a very productive activity). Each body can also move simply for the joy of movement.

When we compare human bodies—male or female—to the bodies of other animals, the human bodies of course are very similar to one another and far different from the bodies of other animals. But when we remove other animals from our field of awareness and focus only on human bodies, we begin to see how starkly different men and women are from each other on a physical level. Anyone can see aspects of this stark difference by walking along any crowded beach or co-ed gym or even a city street on a summer day. In the overwhelming majority of cases, the men's bodies are far more physically powerful than are the women's bodies. This difference is even more stark in comparisons of men and women who have the same parents and/or who engage in similar physical activities. *Ceteris paribus*, men are much more physically powerful than women are.

A woman's body has the potential to gestate and bear children, whether or not the woman actualizes that potential. This fact is not an isolated add-on to the rest of reality; this fact, like all facts, has implications. Whether or not a woman actually bears children, a great deal of a woman's physical energy and overall capacity is spent involuntarily on being ready to bear children, and her body is structured largely for that function. Consequently, a woman's body cannot be as organized structurally as a man's for doing heavy physical work; moreover, a lesser proportion of a woman's physical energy is available for such work.

Here are some particulars. A woman's skin is less resistant than a man's to being broken. In addition to being shaped for bearing children instead of moving external objects, the bones and muscles of a fit woman constitute a lesser proportion of the total weight of a comparably fit man; stated another way, a woman has significantly more body fat. The woman's extra body fat, compared to that of a man, protects her—and any child she might carry—from extremes of temperature. This fat also is shaped to smooth out her form, making her muscles almost invisible, and making her soft to the touch. A woman has breasts for feeding an infant (and/or for being beautiful for a man), but these breasts cannot lift or move anything. For her size, a woman eats less and metabolizes less than a man does. A woman's menstrual cycle consumes a significant amount of her energy. A woman's sources of energy do not give the woman nearly the amounts of physical power and quickness that a man's sources do. A woman has enough strength to move her own body, but proportionally far less than a comparably trained man does to move external things.

The legs of a woman can be strong, though not as strong as a man's can be. Legs are used for locomotion. The woman can move herself—along with a child that she may be gestating—around in the world. The much greater difference between men and women is in the upper body. The upper limbs are for manipulation, for reshaping the environment to further a human's survival.

No matter how small the man, his body is still organized to do physical work to reshape the world. A small man will have less strength than a large man has to move as much of the world in one go, but the small man can make two trips instead of one. However much he can do in one go, any healthy man can do enough to survive. If he does not have the physical power to work well enough to survive, he does not have the physical power for sex.

Moreover, a man's body thrives on physical work. His large bones can take on a range of muscle mass, depending on the specifics of the work he does, without sacrificing speed, flexibility, and other physical virtues. Furthermore, a man's bones are far more resistant to traumatic injury. Whereas a blow to the head of a man might cause damage, the same blow to the head of a woman would be catastrophic.

Of course, in rare cases, a particular large woman is stronger than a particular small man. But the difference between the energy and physical power of a man and a woman is a matter of proportion, not merely absolute amounts. A man has a much greater portion of his energy available for moving things. No matter how physically strong and powerful a woman becomes because she values physical power highly, she knows that a man, *ceteris paribus*, with values similar to hers, can far exceed her in this respect.

From simple observations of multitudes of living creatures, a layman can infer that every living species has an integrity to it: each aspect of a living entity is organized to work in harmony with the other aspects. So too must it be with human men and women. Therefore, without our having to know the specific science on a cellular or molecular level, we can infer that on every physical level from molecular to cellular to organs to the physical whole, men are more organized than women are for physical power.

This inference is not contradicted by the fact that some men, through injury or other disability, are less able than some women are to do heavy physical work. A golf cart might be able to pull a heavier load than a pickup truck can if the truck has four flat tires. But the truck is still the vehicle that is built for power at its core, and the truck can express this power in ways other than pulling a load.

In short, the physical work of moving heavy things or dealing with physical danger is more in harmony with man's physical nature than woman's.

The disparity in physical strength between men and women applies even more categorically to the main sex organs. In sexual arousal, many physical changes occur, but the most dramatic change—in terms of the degree of physical transformation and the degree of sensational urge felt—is in the area of the man's and woman's genital organs. When these areas of the man and woman meet each other, the male organ—the penis—penetrates; the female organ—the vagina—gives way. The ability of one entity physically to move another, or physically to resist movement, is the literal meaning of strength. In this act of sexual intercourse, it is the male's sex organ—the one that penetrates—that is stronger than the one that gives way.

The fact that the stronger sex has the stronger sex organ is no coincidence. The source of a man's muscle power is the same as the source of the power of his sexual arousal. We do not need advanced science—such as knowledge of testosterone and other specific hormones—to know this fact. In both muscular exertion and sexual arousal, the man experiences general excitement, faster heartbeat, and so on; this similarity of response by the body indicates that the source of energy for muscular exertion and for sexual arousal is the same one source. Moreover, if a man needs all his physical power channeled to his muscles, he does not have an erection. Only if he has power to spare does he get an erection. A man's energy does not get channeled into sexual arousal when he needs that energy to move the world. That energy is channeled to sexuality when the moving of the world is done. The fact that a man either heavily exerts his muscles or is aroused sexually, but not both together, also indicates that there is one source of energy for both activities. Therefore, it is not surprising that the man, stronger in bone and muscle, is also stronger in his sex organ.

Thus we have covered the first of the four factors I stated above, namely that men have an inherited physical advantage over women: physical power. Now let us address the second factor by considering the kinds of productive work that men and women can do, and the kinds of work they might choose to do.

Consider this slice of life of a woman in a modern city. The woman awakens in the morning and sees the ceiling. Her house or apartment was built with steel or wood, and bricks. She and other women perhaps could have built it by great struggle and physical hardship. Instead, the home was built by men who thrived on the work. The woman rises and flicks a switch, and light floods the room. The power cables deep underground, the electrical generators, the nuclear power plants, were built by men. With another flick of the wrist, the woman turns on the water faucet. The water that flows traveled through steel water mains deep underground, from powerful rivers dammed by men. The woman lifts a pencil and writes on a sheet of paper—perhaps as part of her professional work—made from trees chopped down by men or cut down by tools made in factories built by men. She turns on the television news and sees a fireman, with heavy tanks and other equipment on his back, climb out of a mine shaft while carrying another man in his arms.

The woman takes an elevator down to the lowest basement level, dug into the ground by men. She drives her car, built in a great factory built by men, through a tunnel under the bed of a great river. The tunnel was built by men. She arrives at an office and shows a group of men and women her plans for a great new bridge, to be erected by men.

Women benefit a great deal from the intermediary of men in their physical dealing with much of the world. A group of men stranded on a desert island or in a wilderness could survive; women would have a much more difficult time if they could survive at all—even though women are just as rational as men are—simply because women lack the physical power of men. Women need men to tame parts of the world for them; women operate within those parts, such as a home or a city.

Of course, women can perform their own enormously challenging physical function that men cannot perform: carrying and bearing children. But regarding their own physical survival, women must trade with men in a way that is equal but not symmetrical. A woman needs a man for the man's strength and for his mind, combined into an ability to face nature alone and to bend it to his will, and to her will too. Nature, to be commanded by woman, requires man to execute the commands. A woman also needs a man for his ability to defend her against evil men. It is good men who make the world safe for and yielding to women. Even in a home or a city, a woman needs the continued presence of good men—most importantly, her man— for the universe to be a benevolent place for her. (See Peikoff 1991, 342 for a discussion of Ayn Rand's term "benevolent universe.")

Moreover, when a woman is pregnant, she cannot fend for herself physically; she needs someone else to protect her. The fact that a woman's body is capable of gestating children is conclusive evidence that a woman's body is not organized to be as physically self-sufficient as a man's. Instead, a woman's body is organized to depend on—yes, depend on—a man.

No matter how technologically advanced a society becomes, so long as human beings remain physical beings, there will always be new adventures that have a significant physical element requiring physical prowess; and so long as the current physical differences between men and women persist, it will always be man who is most able to lead the way in facing those challenges.

Similarly, there will always be physical threats—often from evil men—to the safety of men and women, and it will always be a man— a good man—who is most able to defend against such threats.

A woman does not rue the fact that she must trade with men to make the world benevolent for her. Instead, she celebrates the existence of such men and, above all, her man.

There is much leeway for rational individual preferences; some women may reasonably engage in physical training, diet, or perhaps even drugs to build physical strength. But if a woman goes too far in this direction, then she will sacrifice her physical asset that not only equals, but—in an important respect—surpasses a man's: beauty.

Thus we have completed our discussion of the second factor of my argument: It is rational for both men and women to choose—in their productive work and physical development—to capitalize on the superior physical power of men. And thus we have introduced the third factor in my argument: Women have an inherited physical advantage over men: beauty as an end in itself.

About beauty, Aristotle writes,

> The chief forms of beauty are order and symmetry and definiteness ...[1078b] [*Metaphysics*, Book XIII, Ch. 3]

> ... to be beautiful, a living creature, and every whole made up of parts, must not only present a certain order in its arrangement of parts, but also must be of a certain definite magnitude. Beauty is a matter of size and order ... [1450b][*Poetics*, Ch. 7].

Ayn Rand once said (Binswanger 1986, 48),

> Beauty is a sense of harmony. Whether it's an image, a human face, a body, or a sunset, take the object which you call beautiful, as a unit [and ask yourself]: what parts is it made up of, what are its constituent elements, and are they all harmonious? If they are, the result is beautiful. If there are contradictions and clashes, the result is marred or positively ugly.

Because a woman—for physiological as well as structural reasons—is, *ceteris paribus*, much less strong than a man, it would take a great deal of extra bulk on a woman's slighter frame to give her nearly the same strength as a comparably large and fit man. Such a woman would have unharmonious constituent elements as compared to the man, because the man's body would clearly be much more efficient, versatile, and healthy. The woman's body would be downright ugly. Even if a woman merely moves in the direction of acquiring a man's strength, there comes a point where she begins to sacrifice her beauty.

In my judgment, a woman's beauty shines when she is not doing heavy or dangerous work, and not expressing an ability to do such work. It is no accident that, in ballet, the man lifts the woman, not the reverse. Even when the man dances solo, his movements demonstrate power, agility, and quickness, along with the ability to lift a woman when he chooses to.

Instead of trying to build a male's physical strength onto her female frame, a woman has another option: find a man. If a woman can find and trust someone to protect her when and if she is pregnant, she should be able to find and trust a man to protect her when she is not. In so doing, she will be leveraging her comparatively best physical asset: her beauty. As I will argue below, she will also be leveraging an even greater asset: her rational judgment of men.

However strong a woman is able to make herself without sacrificing her beauty, she will reasonably require a man who is even stronger. That is the only way for her man to concretize for her the value of men—who are better organized than she is for physical power—in making the universe benevolent.

Now that I have discussed the inherited physical advantages of each sex and how to apply those advantages in choices pertaining to productive work and physical development, I will present the fourth factor in my argument: A heterosexual relationship is a further, profound way to capitalize on the physical advantages of each sex.

When I refer to a heterosexual relationship, I refer of course to the entire relationship, not merely the act of sexual intercourse. Indeed, it is the masculine and feminine roles throughout the relationship that lead to the roles in sexual intercourse.

Even when a man and woman are together in a place already tamed by men, such as a home or a city, it is the man who leads in facing any immediate physical danger that might arise. If an ominous sound is heard, it is the man who goes ahead to investigate it. Even in a casual evening ride home on his and her bicycles, it is the man who rides in front. In any instance of facing an immediate danger or potential danger, when there is no time for discussion or joint consideration, the man must decide for himself what to do and then act accordingly, in defense of the woman even more than of himself.

A man must spend a large part of his time and energy training, planning, and acting to anticipate and neutralize any physical threat against his woman. A man must make sure that his woman is safe at all times, and that she knows it. He must make sure she knows that his superior power will always be available to defend her, and never to endanger her.

The requirement that a man have the courage and ability to fight other men—to the death, if necessary—in order to defend the woman he loves (not to mention their children) is such a basic requirement of manhood that it can aptly be called metaphysical. Every young child knows this requirement on some level. Every era of Western culture contains art that portrays this requirement—from the story of the Trojan War to modern pop-culture movies such as *Back to the Future, Braveheart,* and *Transformers,* to children's cartoons such as *Popeye* and *Mighty Mouse.*

The more desirable a woman, the more she will be a target for evil men, and the more courage and ability her man will need to win her and to keep her safe.

A woman needs such a man, a man who is courageous, decisive, and efficacious. To choose such a man, a woman must be a *supreme judge of individual men.*

(Of course, some women—such as some women with military training—are more capable than some men in handling threats from other men. If I fell in love with a woman more capable than I in some of these respects, I would judge myself inadequate for that woman, because clearly she places a high value on these physical abilities that I lack. To be deserving of that woman, I would have to train myself up in the areas in which I was lacking, and I would also have to identify some important respect in which I was the main source of physical power in the relationship.)

A man faces many harsh physical elements in the world at large. His essential asset is his mind, but he also needs his body. As I have discussed, he needs a certain amount of physical strength—guided by his mind, of course—to reshape harsh elements of the world to serve his survival and enjoyment.

A rational man succeeds at this task. It is a difficult, challenging task that requires diverse mental and physical actions, in adherence to the highest moral standards, across wide expanses of place and time.

Then the man faces a woman. The woman exhibits none of the physical harshness or physical resistance that the man encountered in the rest of the world. The woman's body, with its understated musculature (compared to a man's), is the final surrender of the world to the man's power. The woman's body shows no utilitarian function except to be able to move in ways that enable the woman to feed on the strength of the man. The woman exhibits no physical power except the power to move to please the man. However hospitable and beautiful the man has made his own corner of the world, this woman surpasses his work in those respects.

Everything I have written above about the comparison between the bodies of men and women can now be stated essentially in this one paragraph. There are many beautiful things in the world: men, women, horses, dogs, cats, children, landscapes. To a man, a woman's body is the most beautiful physical thing, because it seems to be organized for no utilitarian function other than to please the man. In a heterosexual relationship, the man and woman view their bodies—always guided by their reasoning minds—in this comparative way: the body of the man is for powerful movements to reshape the physical world, whereas the body of the woman is for leveraging the man's power and for moving in such a way as to be beautiful to the man.

Now let us see the intellectual and emotional result of this physical difference.

A woman judges a man as if her life depends on that judgment. Her life *does* depend on that judgment. For a woman, judging a man is the true oldest profession.

A courageous woman chooses to be a judge of men, and to cultivate a body pleasing to men, instead of trying to acquire the physical power of men. For a woman, there is nothing more courageous than to assert herself as a judge of men, and then to trust her judgment to trust a particular man—a soul that far exceeds her in physical power—with her body and her life.

The understated musculature in the woman is not a lack; instead, this understatement accentuates her spiritual power and courage. She brings to the encounter with a man her confidence in her judgment of the man and in her ability to reward him. She has "gone all in" on exploiting her female endowment of beauty and other aspects of her womanhood.

The man that a woman chooses does not have to be the best man in terms of physical power isolated from other attributes of men. He *does* have to be the best man in terms of his combination of mind and body according to the woman's personal values. This combination must contain some element of the physical as well as the mental, so that the woman can experience the physical combined with the mental power of man. Her man is not just her partner John (or Frank or Joe); he is her *man* John. For her, he is the best man among men.

For a man, it is marvelous, or terrifying, to behold another soul— in a much weaker body, because the soul has eschewed physical power in favor of utmost beauty—that has the audacity yet to face the man proudly and, through her actions, pronounce judgment on him.

Of course, both man and woman must judge everything, including each other. But there is something about a woman judging a man that is more intense, more focused, more elevated, more solemn, more audacious, more central to the very existence of the judge. To a man, the mind of a woman is the purest essence of judgment. The woman is judging whether the man is fit for—and worthy of—survival. The woman is also judging whether the man is fit to be the woman's primary defense against all physical threats from nature and other men.

In short, a woman judges the metaphysical worth of a man. The man that a woman judges to be worthy of her becomes part of her metaphysics.

For a man, Judgment Day is every day that he is naked—in body and spirit—before a woman. The proud, courageous man embraces this test. The coward hides from it. The proud, courageous man seeks the judge with the highest standards. The coward seeks the lowest, or no judge at all.

The woman's inviting body and stern mind express the challenge, "Show me how you have shaped the world, and I will judge your work." Romance for a man is his meeting of this challenge. Romance is his condensed reenactment of his lifelong course of having shaped the world into a form most auspicious to his life. But there is another, most crucial form of condensation that romance provides: the woman's body is connected to the woman's mind, a mind that understands *conceptually* the meaning of all the diverse and dispersed actions taken by the man over the course of his life.

Thus the woman is more than simply a metaphorical "mirror" for the man. The man sees, in the woman, more than just a reflection of his own character traits. The man sees a condensation, through his effect on the consciousness and body of the woman, of the entirety of his effect on the world.

The term "benevolent universe," as Ayn Rand uses it (Peikoff 1991, 342), is a kind of metaphor, a personification; the universe does not literally have a mental attitude toward man. To a man, a woman is that aspect of the universe about which the phrase "benevolent universe" is most literal. The universe has no mind with which to pass judgment on the man, but the woman does.

As a man sees his effect on the woman, the woman sees her effect on the man, and she as well takes pride in this result. The relationship between the man and woman is reciprocal, but not symmetrical. The woman does not construe her effect on the man as the sum of her effect on the world. Rather she sees her effect on the man alone, who in turn affects the world.

In other words, the man conquers the woman as he conquered the world. The woman enchants the man who conquered the world.

Now let us consider the physical contact involved in romance.

In my judgment, romantic physical contact—or physical touch— should go through three chronological stages: loving touch, sensual touch, sexual (erotic) touch. Each of these successive stages should include the elements of the preceding stage, plus a new element.

The first stage, loving touch, might continue for many months before progressing to the next stage. This stage might be—and perhaps should be—the only stage that occurs before marriage.

A loving touch can take many forms: the touch of an arm, holding hands, walking arm in arm, a hug, a kiss. No matter the form, a loving touch should be accompanied by thoughts of love. The style of a loving touch should suggest the ideas mentioned above. That is, the man should touch the woman with the firmness to demonstrate his power to conquer the world, and the gentleness to demonstrate his commitment to safeguard the woman.

In the next stage, sensual touch, the man takes delight in the physical beauty of what he is touching. In this stage, all the elements of the previous stage of loving touch should remain; otherwise, the pleasure of the sensual stage would be shallow and fleeting. This stage is very intimate, and should occur only in private. No one but the man and woman constituting the loving couple has earned the right to share in this stage in any way, not even as an observer.

The sexual/erotic stage is even more intimate, of course. And just as the thoughts and feeling of the loving stage must persist during the sensual stage, so the thoughts and feelings of the loving and sensual stages must persist in the sexual/erotic stage. The greatest joy, even during sexual intercourse, comes from the elements of the loving stage. Indeed, without the loving stage and sensual stage, sexual contact is detrimental, not beneficial. The following description of sexual/erotic contact assumes the persistence of the elements of loving and sensual contact.

Sexual arousal in a man is a surge of power. Sexual arousal in a woman is a surge of hunger for the man's power.

The man leads. The woman judges the man's lead and decides whether to follow in her own way. Again, the relationship is not symmetrical, but it is balanced—between two souls of equal stature. The woman's judging is as intellectually demanding and as independent as the man's leading. There is no sterner, more ruthless judge of a man than a heroine. There is no challenge requiring more strength of character from a man than to win and keep the heroine. If you don't believe me, ask Howard Roark (the hero in Ayn Rand's novel, *The Fountainhead*).

Of course, the man judges the woman too. But that judgment is a preliminary, a qualifying round, the ticket for the woman's admission to the main event that is sexual intercourse. Unlike friendship or many working relationships, or even some (though not all) aspects of a loving relationship, sexual intercourse has an essential physical component. Because of this essential physical component, it must be the man who is in charge; the man is in command, and the woman judges his command.

In a modern economy, there is much division of labor among men, and also among men and women. But in sex, the man cannot delegate the use of physical power to another man, or to power tools, or to the woman. The job is the man's alone. Similarly, the job of being beautiful is the woman's alone.

Sexual arousal in a man is an emotional call to express his strength and power to a worthy judge. Consistent with the other aspects of being a man is the physical nature of his arousal: his sex organ becomes hard and strong. The man feels an intense physical urge that can be satisfied only by entering the woman with that organ. Being inside the softer woman with his hard sex organ is an expression of power and strength of the man toward the woman, combined with profound love and intense physical pleasure.

Sexual arousal in a woman is an emotional response based on her evaluation—her judgment—of the man. Her arousal is an emotional call to feed on the spiritual and physical power of the man.

The man dominates—yet always protects, as with his loving touch—the woman. He overwhelms her with his physical power at the command of his spiritual power. Dominance is not a matter of activity over passivity; both souls are fully active. Dominance is irrespective of relative physical elevation or relative amount of physical motion. Even if the woman at times might seem to be more active or aggressive, it is so only because the man entertains her efforts. There is never any question of which individual is the more powerful, of who is really in charge, of who is feeding power to whom. If such a question does arise, the celebration is transformed into contempt, humiliation, and mutual despair. For this reason, sex roles must never be reversed.

There is plenty of room in this encounter for originality on the part of the woman, but always within the safe environment created and defended by—and always at the pleasure of—the man.

The foregoing does not preclude, in the least, the man being emotionally available. Emotional availability does not imply physical or mental weakness. I do not think that men are organized to feel less than women do. But men may feel less *often* than women do. That is because, in times of physical crisis, which men face more often than women do, human beings must channel most of their energy to outward action, not to heavy releases of emotion. As the man acts against the harsh elements of the world, the woman often is freed to release her energy in the form of emotion. Later, when the danger has passed and the man and woman are together, the man can release his energy as emotion too. At the times when a woman too is required to act in a crisis—such as a danger to the health of a child— she too is not overwhelmed by emotion; her emotions flow later, when the danger is past.

The man is hard, strong, unbending, decisive, the leader, the champion, the protector, the physically dominant one, the indomitable. The woman is soft, supple, eager, challenging, judgmental. ("Yes" means "good.") The man asserts his power; the woman clutches it and feeds on it. The man dominates and conquers; the woman judges and surrenders. The man's actions say, "This is how I face nature alone, and command it, for myself and for you. For my success, you are my highest reward." The woman's actions say, "Yes. I approve! I commend my self to you, my champion." All of this is combined with intense, simultaneous, and fully satisfying physical pleasure, as each soul's aroused anatomical organs conjoin.

In short, the man leads and dominates; the woman challenges and judges. Such is the nature of sexual intercourse between a man and woman.

Now we are ready to introduce the concepts of masculinity and femininity. The essence of masculinity is rational, decisive, indomitable leadership. The essence of femininity is the passion to judge individual men, and to find one man that lives up to the woman's highest standards.

In other words, the man is the executive, and the woman is the judiciary. There is no legislature, because the laws come from reality, and they set requirements for romantic love and sex.

Clearly, the concepts of masculinity and femininity entail the integration of mind and body. Why then is the title of the present book *Masculine Power, Feminine Beauty*, a title that emphasizes the physical elements of masculinity and femininity? The reason is that the physical elements are the factual basis upon which men choose to develop masculine values and women choose to develop feminine values. There are no innate ideas. A woman's mind is not born with a desire to focus on judging men, and a man's mind is not born with a desire to focus on taming the world. These values develop in rational men and women as rational conclusions based on a rational assessment of each individual's own abilities.

Some writers on the subject of sexual orientation use the word "complementarity" to denote complementary functions of the man and woman in procreation. In contrast, I am arguing for much more than that. An entity's nature encompasses all of the entity's characteristics, which are causally connected and form a whole. Because of this integrity of an entity's nature, the complementarity of man and woman is pervasive, transcending the complementarity in procreation, and encompassing the entirety of the physical and spiritual needs of the man and woman in their romantic, sexual relationship.

Some may argue that my theory places too much pressure on the man to perform. Well, that is life, and life is good. Sexual intercourse is a physical act as well as a spiritual one. The physical world requires performance. In the untamed world, one bad performance brings death. That is why a man needs self-esteem, which brings confidence. A man who lacks confidence cannot perform sexually or in any other way. But to a confident man, the need to perform is not pressure; it is adventure.

In rare cases, individuals are born anatomically ambiguous in terms of their sex. Such instances are simply borderline cases and as such have no philosophical significance to my theory. Just as those who argue in favor of homosexuality and/or subjectivity in sexual orientation do not restrict their advocacy to such borderline cases but attempt to apply their ideas to clear cases as well—to cases of physically healthy individuals with unambiguous sexual anatomies—so I too address such clear cases.

As I have indicated, it is possible for a woman to embark on a regimen of drugs, diet, and exercise that could make her more and more physically like a man. She can even take the ultimate step of surgically changing herself. Consistent with my theory, I am not attracted to such individuals.

In summary, in a heterosexual romantic relationship, the man and the woman both leverage their biological advantages in such a way as to celebrate their efficacy in a benevolent universe.

A man can gather strength from the friendship and love of another man. But such an interaction is a means to an end, a preparation for each man to go on and triumph in his own life. In contrast, sexual intercourse is an end in itself, a man's triumph. In sex, there are two individuals, but each man is a man alone, triumphing on his own, on the basis of his power alone. Similarly, each woman is a woman alone, triumphing on her own, on the basis of her judgment and beauty alone.

Once the romantic partners realize that the depth of the relationship reaches a certain threshold, then the partners realize that the relationship must be permanent. At that time, the man and woman are ready to marry and, if they choose, to have children.

The causal chain is as follows: First, the man and woman in love are ready to make their romance permanent, enshrined by marriage; then, as an effect, they are also ready to be good parents if they choose to have children. This causal chain is recognized by our culture's traditional marriage vows, which speak of lifelong honor and devotion between husband and wife but make no mention of children. Fidelity to the woman he loves is what leads a rational man to take the vow of marriage. This vow is a wonderful conceptualization of the depth of love and devotion between husband and wife.

I hope that my account in this chapter will motivate others to write on the subject of heterosexual romantic love with objectivity, as I have strived to do.

2. THE ROLE OF VOLITION IN SEXUAL ORIENTATION

The previous chapter presented a constellation of physical facts about how men differ from women. These facts then were used to explain why a heterosexual romantic relationship is so fulfilling. The present chapter explains that the causal connection from physical facts to sexual orientation consists not of biological determinism, but of *volition*. That is, the constellation of physical facts about men and women plays a crucial role in sexual orientation: not in determining sexual orientation, but in being a basic aspect of reality that each mind recognizes, considers, and evaluates, thereby leading to a sexual orientation.

Love is in part an emotional response. In my judgment, sexual attraction and arousal also are, at least to a significant degree, emotional responses. Therefore, to understand the role of volition in sexual orientation, it is important to understand the role of volition in emotions.

Volition and Emotions

We do not directly choose any of our emotional responses. But we do make prior, more basic choices that in turn cause our emotional responses.

Consider the case of millions of Americans listening to a speech by former U.S. President Obama. Half of the listeners might be moved to pleasurable tears. A few might feel a thrill up their leg. The other half of the audience might feel loathing and contempt. Does any individual choose his particular emotional reaction to the former president? No, the emotion erupts automatically. Are these diverse emotional responses caused by differences in genetics? Of course not; such a claim would be racist. Are the diverse responses caused by society? No, emotional reactions to the former president cut across all social groups.

Our emotional responses to Obama are caused by our prior judgments, our prior evaluation of whether he is good for us and the things we value dearly, or bad for us and the things we value dearly. Sometime in our past, we made evaluations not only of the former president, but also of what things in the world are important to us. All of these prior evaluations are choices.

On a recent anniversary of D-Day, I attended a reception for U.S. veterans of World War II and the Korean War. When we sang "God Bless America," many of the veterans and guests were moved to tears. Did we choose to weep at that moment? Of course not. But sometime in our past, we made judgments about our country and about the men and women who fight for it, and about the importance of those things to us. Those past judgments are the cause of our present tears when we honor our military heroes.

I do not remember when I made the judgment that America is a great nation, worth fighting for, worth risking death for, and something I could not live without. But I know that I made the judgment, because I still hold it today.

We all can recall many times when we struggled to hold back tears or hold in laughter. We did not choose to have these emotions; indeed, we were trying to choose not to have them. The emotions were there, automatically. But the emotions reflected our own, personal, chosen values. We may not remember when we chose those values. We may have chosen them at a very young age. But we chose them.

These examples illustrate a ubiquitous phenomenon: All of our emotional responses, though automatic in the present, are caused by our values chosen in the past. The same pattern—chosen evaluation followed by emotional response—applies to the emotions related to romantic love and sexual attraction.

Volition, Romantic Love, and Sexual Attraction

Romantic love entails one person's "sense-of-life" response to the "sense of life" of another person. (A sense of life is a crucial kind of emotional response, which will be described below.) This emotional aspect of love is experienced in the present as automatic and non-volitional. But love has two volitional elements, as described by Ayn Rand. (See for example, Ayn Rand [1966] 1975). First, emotions—though experienced as automatic—are based on prior value judgments, which were made volitionally. Second, it is possible to identify the prior value judgments and reaffirm (or reject) these judgments in the present, based on explicit, volitional reasoning. Reaffirming these judgments makes love an integration of reason and emotion, of mind and body.

Here is some of Ayn Rand's ([1966] 1975, 25–26) writing on the matter.

> A sense of life is a pre-conceptual equivalent of metaphysics, an emotional, subconsciously integrated appraisal of man's relationship to existence.
>
> ...
>
> Long before he is old enough to grasp such a concept as metaphysics, man makes choices, forms value-judgments, experiences emotions and acquires a certain *implicit* view of life. Every choice and value-judgment implies some estimate of himself and of the world around him—most particularly, of his capacity to deal with the world.
>
> ...
>
> To the extent to which a man is mentally active, *i.e.,* motivated by the desire to know, to *understand,* his mind works as the programmer of his emotional computer—and his sense of life develops into a bright counterpart of a rational philosophy. To the extent to

which a man evades, the programming of his emotional
computer is done by chance influences: by random im-
pressions, associations, imitations, by undigested
snatches of environmental bromides, by cultural osmo-
sis.

Thus a man can allow society to shape his emotional responses.
Statistically, many men do so, and that is a main reason why many
people in a given society have similar emotional responses. But this
statistical fact does not mean that society caused such a man's emotions; the man *chose*--often by default, by not choosing to exert the
mental effort to think for himself—to go along with society. A man
can choose otherwise; he can choose to use his own reasoning, and
some men do.

Similarly, a man can allow his subconscious mind's automatic associations to shape his emotional responses. But again, this allowing
is a choice. Alternatively, a man can choose to focus his mind to form
conceptual groupings, and these chosen conceptual groupings will
preempt automatic associations as the main shapers of his emotional
responses.

Later in the same article ([1966] 1975, 30–31), Ayn Rand writes,

If his mind does not provide him with a comprehensive
view of existence, his sense of life will. ... [F]or good or
evil (and, usually, for evil), he is left at the mercy of a
subconscious philosophy which he does not know, has
never checked, has never been aware of accepting.

Many individuals report that they do not recall choosing a sexual
orientation. Nor does one recall choosing a sense of life, or any emotional response. But throughout his life, an individual evaluates every
experience, and programs his emotions based on the sum of those
evaluations. Each one of those evaluations is a choice.

Later, Ayn Rand ([1966] 1975, 32) writes,

> ... a sense of life is *not* an irreducible primary, but a very
> complex sum; it can be felt, but it cannot be under-
> stood, by an automatic reaction; to be understood, it
> has to be analyzed, identified and verified conceptually.
> ...
>
> There are two aspects of man's existence which are the
> special province and expression of his sense of life: love
> and art. I am referring here to romantic love, in the se-
> rious meaning of that term ...

In the previous chapter, I explored the aspect of a sense of life that
responds romantically to someone from the opposite sex.

As a sense of life can seem like an irreducible primary, so can a
person's emotional response to certain works of art, and so can romantic love. But as a sense of life can and should be verified conceptually, so too with romantic love. Ayn Rand ([1966] 1975, 32) continues,

> Love is a response to values. It is with a person's sense
> of life that one falls in love—with that essential sum,
> that fundamental stand or way of facing existence,
> which is the essence of a personality.

Then there is the quotation (Rand [1966] 1975, 33) I referenced
in my introduction:

> Love is *the expression of philosophy*—of a subconscious
> philosophical sum—and, perhaps, no other aspect of
> human existence needs the *conscious* power of philoso-
> phy quite so desperately.

As with romantic love, so it is with sex, an integral aspect of romantic love. Ayn Rand writes (1957, 489–490 [Part 2, Chapter 4]),

> The men who think that wealth comes from material
> resources and has no intellectual root or meaning, are

the men who think—for the same reason—that sex is a
physical capacity which functions independently of
one's mind, choice or code of values. They think that
your body creates a desire and makes a choice for
you—just about in some such way as if iron ore transformed itself into railroad rails of its own volition. Love
is blind, they say; sex is impervious to reason and
mocks the power of all philosophers. But, in fact, a
man's sexual choice is the result and the sum of his fundamental convictions. Tell me what a man finds sexually attractive and I will tell you his entire philosophy
of life. Show me the woman he sleeps with and I will
tell you his valuation of himself.

A woman does not choose to be aroused by a heroic man and
turned off by a scoundrel, or vice versa, but those reactions occur
based on prior, chosen evaluations of her own moral worth. Some
people are sexually attracted only to one man or woman—their
spouse, their highest personal value.

Even sexual responses to physical features are based on chosen
values. When I began to study dance and admire the grace of female
dancers, I became attracted to women with lithe bodies, down shoul-
ders, and long necks; that is, my attraction to certain physical features developed as my knowledge and values developed. Some
women are attracted to a heavily-muscled physique, some to a sleek
physique, some to a pudgy body; these various attractions are reflec-
tive of the woman's personality and personal chosen values. These
choices are not necessarily moral choices, but they are choices.

Just as many men are not aware of making a choice to be attracted
to heroines or sluts, and they are not aware of choosing to succeed
or to fail to "perform" when encountering the kind of beautiful
woman they profess to desire, and just as many women are not aware
of making a choice to be attracted to "bad boys" or to men of high

social status, or to men of high moral character, so many individuals are not aware of making a choice of sexual orientation.

Heterosexual men sometimes are not aroused by a woman even when they want to be. The condition under this circumstance is called erectile dysfunction. Sometimes the cause is biological/environmental—such as fatigue, alcohol, or lack of food. But often the cause is psychological, such as anxiety or fear in a certain circumstance. Some men cannot be aroused whenever they are in bed with any woman for the first time. Such men don't remember ever choosing to have this condition (which is not necessarily a bad condition); they just seem to have it. So how could it be a choice? The answer is that they feel cautious in the current situation, based on evaluations they made in the past—perhaps far in the past—in associated circumstances.

A man aroused by the sight of a beautiful woman may lose his arousal when he learns that she is a mere teenager, or when he hears her immature voice. A man's attraction to someone who looks like a woman may turn to revulsion when the man learns that the other person is really a man. A twelve-year-old boy could be attracted to beautiful twelve-year-old old girls but not to beautiful fifty-year-old women. When the boy becomes a mature middle-aged man, his responses are the reverse. Again, sexuality is based on values.

Everyone knows that young children can be sexually aroused by many things, such as touching their genitals, or swishing water in a bathtub, or physical play. For adults, out-of-context arousal can occur in many forms, like other out-of-context emotions. A man can be aroused by a teenage girl until he remembers the context of her age. It has been documented that victims of rape often are sexually aroused during the horrible act (Levin and Berlo, 2004). This fact does not imply that the victims should seek more rape. Even objects accidentally rubbed up against the body can cause arousal. These facts have little or no significance.

Sexuality is more than a physical phenomenon. A sexual response is not merely the response of one body to another body. The response is not caused merely by some gene or hormone that automatically triggers one body to feel pleasure from the look or feel of another body. A sexual response is the result of one person's evaluation of the combination of mind and body of the other person and of oneself. These evaluations are choices.

In short, sexuality includes an individual's cognition, values, and evaluation.

Volition and Sex-Specific Sexual Attraction

My first interest in a girl, for her being a girl, was at age five. By that time, I already had a rich conception of men, women, and the relation between them, along with an understanding that I would grow into a man and that the girls I saw would grow into women. Indeed, my interest in this particular girl began with my likening her behavior to the behavior of appealing grown women I had observed. Moreover, important elements of my sense of life were already in place. All of these conceptions and elements are of course laden with choices and evaluations. By age twelve, when I experienced my first sexual interest in a girl, of course my conceptions and evaluations of men, women, and myself were much more developed.

My experience of sexual interest or arousal toward a woman is never in the form of a primitive sensation—such as a scent of a woman, or a voice of a woman, or the softness of a woman's skin, or a distinctive female shape—apart from the conceptual identification that this sensation is coming to me from a woman. I might find these sensations pleasurable as isolated sensations, but they do not bring sexual interest or arousal unless I also identify that they are emanating from a woman. Even at a purely physical level, the sexual appeal of a woman for me always requires a conceptual component: the conceptual identification that this human being is a woman. A conceptual identification requires volition—specifically, the volitional

2. The Role of Volition in Sexual Orientation

placing of a mental unit into a certain group of mental units. For the same reason, volition is also involved in evaluating—as good for me or bad for me—something I identify conceptually.

There is no reason to think that sex-specific sexual attraction is any less volitional than are sexual attraction to youth or maturity, to genius or dullness, to security or danger, to strength or weakness, to success or failure, to virtue or vice, to stoutness or slenderness, to muscular bulk or muscular sleekness. Some of these alternatives have moral implications, and some are morally neutral but are expressions of personality. None of these feelings of attraction are chosen directly; but they proceed from values, which are the result of choices.

In the previous chapter, I explained my own values and emotions regarding sex-specific sexual evaluation. I identified—in explicit, conceptual terms—why I am sexually attracted to women. (In the next chapter, I will explain why I am repulsed by the idea of sexual contact with men.) Coming to understand these values and emotions of mine in the philosophical terms I have presented here has enhanced my life. Whether one shares my ideas or objects to them, one should be able to explain *his* values and emotions.

What does heterosexuality say about a man's values and philosophy of life? A heterosexual man stands solely on his own power and efficacy, which he knows has earned him the beauty of a woman who demands the best from him and judges him accordingly.

Of course, much work is to be done to identify precisely how specific choices—and what kind of choices—lead to sex-specific sexual values even before an individual is mature and self-aware enough to consider these choices in a deliberative, philosophical manner. Upon reflecting on my own past, I can state the following. Even as a child, I found females beautiful. I could think that a man or boy was handsome, but women and girls were beautiful. Even then, I had a sense that women were a more pure embodiment of beauty. As an adult, I can express the sense I had in these terms: Feminine beauty is a kind of beauty that, compared to masculine beauty, is less utilitarian and more of an end in itself.

Also, when interacting with a girl, I sensed that I was on my own, that everything was up to me, that it was my responsibility to be in charge and to be judged for it. In this respect, I was probably informed by Western culture's healthy tradition of the man being the woman's champion. This responsibility was daunting. For me, individual choices to face and assert myself with girls required resolve in the face of fear, and such choices preceded by many years my sexual attraction to anyone.

Throughout her writing on romantic love, Ayn Rand implicitly refers to love between a man and a woman. All the evidence indicates that she considered heterosexuality an obvious prerequisite for—not merely an optional feature of—romantic love. For example, she writes ([1968] 1990, 51),

> To classify the unique emotion of *romantic love* as a form of *friendship* is to obliterate it: the two emotional categories are mutually exclusive. The feeling of friendship is asexual; it can be experienced toward a member of one's own sex.

Nevertheless, Ayn Rand does not explicitly address, in her writing, sexual orientation. Despite my extensive quoting of Ayn Rand and my reliance on her ideas on romantic love, I make no claim that she would have agreed with my theory presented herein regarding sex-specific sexual values.

3. JUDGING HOMOSEXUALITY—IF THE LAW WILL ALLOW IT

A basic, inescapable physical fact is that two men or two women cannot conceive a child.

The inability ever to conceive children together is a terrible hardship for most reasonable individuals. Although a romantic couple might reasonably choose at a particular time not to have children, a heterosexual couple is not bound to such a constraint permanently. But a homosexual couple is bound to such a constraint so long as the couple remains a couple.

Adoption is an alternative to conception, but it is an alternative not always available. Adoption requires someone else's failure or hardship: an unwanted birth. The more prosperous a society, the rarer such failures or hardships. That is why so many adoptions today in the United States are of children born in less prosperous societies.

Moreover, an adopting couple misses out on the process of conception, gestation, and birth, and on the period of time from birth to adoption.

The same shortcomings, for the most part, apply to artificial insemination involving an outsider.

Another basic, inescapable physical fact is that the primary sexually aroused anatomical parts of two men or two women do not fit together. (This physical fact is one of the "elephants in the room," which I will discuss later, that seem to be taboo in contemporary academic writings in support of homosexuality.) Two men or two women are unable to experience coitus. Coitus is the most intimate, visible (in the sense of each partner being physically and spiritually visible to the other), and intense expression of romantic love. If

anyone doubts this fact, consider what it would be like for a heterosexual couple to have to forego this form of sexual bonding; that
would be nothing short of a tragedy. The nonpareil value of coitus—
even in the absence of a desire to have children—is the reason why
contraception is so highly valued by so many; that is, for coitus, many
couples are willing to risk even an unwanted pregnancy.

Yes, there are forms of sexual contact other than coitus, but they
are all secondary to coitus in intimacy, visibility, and intensity. To
healthy heterosexuals, such other forms are mere foreplay if engaged
in at all.

In our advanced society, most heterosexuals develop their sexual
orientation before experiencing or contemplating various forms of
sexual contact; only later do these individuals learn of and come to
value most highly the one form of sexual contact that turns out to be
unavailable to homosexuals. That is, individuals become heterosexual not because they value coitus. Similarly, individuals become homosexual not because they value other forms of sexual contact more
than coitus. Therefore, it is reasonable to conclude that the inability
to experience coitus diminishes the sexual fulfillment of homosexuals as much as such an inability would diminish the sexual fulfillment
of heterosexuals. Indeed, the grain of truth in the "transgender"
movement is the realization that complementarity of sex organs is
important.

Yes, homosexuals can still have some kind of sex life, as people
without hands can learn to grasp with their toes. Nevertheless, on the
physical level, the form of sexual contact available to homosexuals is
so severely impoverished that it could aptly be called crippled. If you
are a heterosexual, you might ask yourself what is more important to
you: the use of a leg or the ability to have coitus.

My words may seem harsh, but they are no harsher than reality.
The high stakes require that I be frank and not mince words. At stake
are not only the feelings of adult homosexuals, but also the disposi-
tion of children being indoctrinated in schools by LGBT (Lesbian,

Gay, Bisexual, Transgender) ideology (see, for example, Pullmann 2019), and of children being raised by homosexual couples. (For an explanation and analysis of LGBT ideology, see especially Chapter 5.) Although adults do not cause children to be homosexual, adults can convey misinformation and expose children to a skewed set of experiences, forming a basis upon which children might make misinformed evaluations that lead to homosexuality. And although many young homosexuals become heterosexual later in life, making that change can be very difficult.

In Chapter 1, I wrote that, in sex, there are two individuals, but each man is a man alone, triumphing on his own, on the basis of his power alone. (Similarly, each woman is a woman alone, triumphing on her own, on the basis of her judgment and beauty alone.) Such a solitary triumph is not possible if there are two men involved in a sexual act. But there is something much worse about sexual intercourse between two men. A man needs to know that he is indomitable. The notion of dominating another man, or being dominated by someone—as the highest form of pleasure and spiritual fulfillment— is a betrayal of every ounce of a man's being. The matter is not primarily one of physical attraction or repulsion, but of man's need for self-esteem.

To a man who seeks his highest pleasure from the power of another man, the healthy emotional response from the other man, if he is heterosexual, is an equivalent of the rebuke, "Be a man! Go forth and claim your birthright!" To a man who would seek such pleasure by exerting his power over another man, the response from a heterosexual man is, "Don't try it on me if you value your life." Each response is imbued with contempt, loathing, and perhaps pity.

Nor could there be any alternating of dominance between two heterosexual men. That would just be alternating between two forms of spiritual debasement and torture, between the roles of master and slave.

I suspect that it is no coincidence that the culture that produced the concept of causality (the concept that entities—such as men and women—have a nature and act in accordance with that nature), produced the concept of individual rights, and abolished slavery is the culture that developed highly stylized, romantic ideals of both masculinity and femininity, each with equally high intellectual and moral stature. And it is no surprise that such a culture developed a healthy aversion to homosexuality.

As for lesbians, they are forlorn of experiencing the most intimate physical contact of coitus or the full human efficacy and power that comes from man.

It is conceivable that my own, personal response to homosexuality could change if I understood a rational theory of homosexual love, if there is one. Indeed, my present aversion to homosexuality developed as I developed an understanding of my heterosexuality. But a rational theory of homosexual love does not consist of the claim that sexual orientation is a matter of determinism or unexplained preference.

What principles, then, should guide a heterosexual in his dealings with homosexuals?

First, individual rights are absolute. Consenting adults have an absolute right to engage in any sexual practices they choose, and they have the right to do anything in public that does not infringe on the rights of other.

Second, being a homosexual does not preclude an individual from being moral and productive. Everyone knows homosexuals who do excellent work and are worthy friends. (The same is true about individuals who are in no romantic or sexual relationship at all, or individuals who have suffered the tragedy of losing a spouse.) Instead of integrating their ideas, individuals can compartmentalize, holding true premises in some aspects of their lives while holding mistaken premises in other aspects.

Sexuality is an end in itself, not necessarily a means to an end. One consequence of this fact is that an unfulfilling sex life may not lead to dysfunctions in other aspects of an individual's life, particularly aspects related to productive work. Though productive work is required for a fulfilling sex life, the reverse is not necessarily so. The penalty—a very heavy penalty indeed—for unwise sexual choices is an unfulfilling sex life, plus the bitter knowledge of that fact and an attendant profound disappointment, but not necessarily an inability to think, work, and achieve some degree of happiness.

Statistically, individuals with unfulfilling sex lives might be more likely to choose self-destructive behavior such as drug abuse or suicide, but all individuals remain free to choose otherwise.

Third, the choices that set an individual's sex-specific sexual evaluations might be made when the individual is very young. Tragically, a child may have little way of knowing that seemingly small choices can be important, that such choices when added together can shape his entire view of the world and his place in it. An individual should not be condemned morally, and perhaps not even criticized morally, for such early choices.

Fourth, recall these words from *Atlas Shrugged* by Ayn Rand (1957, 490 [Part 2, Chapter 4]):

> Observe the ugly mess which most men make of their
> sex lives ...

If one had to limit his professional dealings by dealing only with people with exemplary sex lives, one might not be able to do much business. Indeed, I am not offering up my own sexual history for public scrutiny. (I wish I knew forty or more years ago what I am writing in the first few chapters of this book.)

Nevertheless, certain policies for a heterosexual's dealings with homosexuals are rationally advisable.

For the enjoyment of beauty untainted by reminders of ugliness, and for the maintenance of one's own healthy sense of life, it is rational to seek out beauty and to avoid ugliness, to seek out instances of joy and to avoid immersion in suffering.

For example, awareness of the death of others is a part of life, but I do not put photos of cadavers up on my walls. Individuals have a right to make ugly "art" and even to show it in their store fronts or on their tee shirts, or to play ugly music; but I can limit my exposure to such ugliness by not allowing it on my property, not going to the wrong galleries or concerts, and not socializing with people who display such ugliness.

For the same reason that it is rational to avoid ugly art, it is rational for a heterosexual to minimize witnessing homosexual displays of affection and any other expressions of homosexuality. Indeed, the greatest cost to me in writing the essay that became this book came from having to conjure images of homosexual interaction. Periodically returning to thoughts about heterosexual interaction was a good antidote. Nevertheless, I was concerned that I was harming myself; when I finished writing the essay, I took time to surround myself with beauty.

To concretize my conclusion, here are some specific policies I would follow except under unusual circumstances. (Such unusual circumstances might include having a son or daughter who is homosexual.) I would not have a homosexual roommate. I would not rent an apartment in my private home to a homosexual. I probably would not have a homosexual business partner that I had to work with closely. I would not vacation with a homosexual or "double date" with a homosexual couple. I certainly would not hire a homosexual psychotherapist.

For children, this issue is more critical. I would not have a homosexual babysitter for my child. I would not hire a homosexual to teach elementary school or to be a camp counselor. Above all, if I had any say in the matter, I would not place a child in the custody of a homosexual individual or couple.

As I argued in Chapter 2, and will continue to argue in Chapter 4, available evidence indicates that an individual's sexual orientation is based primarily on the individual's choices. Often, such choices—which include early yet elaborate conceptions and evaluations of boys, girls, men, and women—are made at a young age, and the resultant emotional patterns are difficult to reverse. Therefore, misleading a child to make choices leading to homosexuality is tantamount to misleading an innocent and ignorant child to becoming a sexual cripple for life. Therefore, at least one prerequisite for a homosexual to be a responsible parent would be for such a parent to avoid suggesting or implying in any way that homosexuality is as auspicious to human life and happiness as is heterosexuality. Unfortunately, few homosexuals would even attempt to avoid such a suggestion or implication, because the vast majority of homosexuals—if statements by homosexuals in the media are representative of the wider population—assert flatly that homosexuality is just as good as heterosexuality.

But even if a homosexual parent did want to avoid suggesting or implying to a young child that homosexuality is just fine, could the parent do so when the parent's own actions implicitly endorse homosexuality? I think not. A man with no hands who eats with his feet does not imply to a child that the child should do likewise, because the child readily sees the man's handicap; but a child does not know about the handicap of incompatible sex organs.

The problem with homosexual parenting, however, is much deeper than the physical handicap intrinsic to homosexuality. Being an expression of values, sexuality is spiritual as well as physical. It is on the spiritual level that homosexuality is most problematic, for homosexuals themselves and also for any children in their household who witness homosexual affectation or affection. As I explained in Chapter 1, the physical difference between men and women is an essential element upon which heterosexual romantic love is built, integrating all aspects of man and woman. A boy developing his masculinity needs to experience his sexuality as an expression of indomitable power and leadership offered to another individual—a woman—who is organized to receive that power, judge that leadership, and thrive on both. For such a boy to witness a relationship in which one man receives power and leadership from another man—or in which neither man is leader—is to witness a perversion of masculinity and what would be a betrayal of masculinity if the boy were to follow in the men's footsteps. To be immersed in witnessing such an emasculating relationship for an entire childhood is a living nightmare. The situation is similar for a girl developing her femininity, witnessing a relationship of two women who will never feel their lover inside them, and never feel a man's physical power and efficacy—a physical power and efficacy that women lack but that is needed to command nature.

If sexual orientation is based on choices, it does not follow that sexual orientation is a moral issue; but deciding on who should adopt a child is indeed a moral issue. From a legal perspective, the moral decision should be made by the natural parents or the natural parents' designated agent—such as an adoption agency designated by the parent—not government.

Many of these policies I recommend are illegal in the United States today. Government can confiscate an individual's property and deny his liberty simply because he refuses to have economic or social intercourse with a homosexual. Government can prohibit biological parents and adoption agencies from discriminating, as is their moral right, against homosexual adopters. These laws are blatant violations of the individual rights of liberty and property. Academia, the mainstream news media, and popular culture are virtual monoliths in support of such vicious laws.

Many homosexual political activists openly take credit for instigating such laws. These laws often do not explicitly mention homosexuals. Instead, the laws simply obliterate the right of individuals to make judgments based on sex-specific sexual values.

Then there are laws and regulations such as this one:

> CIC Section 10291.5(c)(2) requires that all applications
> for health insurance (excluding guaranteed issue)
> prominently display the following notice: "California
> law prohibits an HIV test from being required or used
> by health insurance companies as a condition of ob-
> taining health insurance coverage."

Keep in mind that since 1985, when a blood test for AIDS was discovered and put to use in the United States, AIDS could be avoided—except in very rare cases—simply by refraining from two barbaric activities: promiscuous sex and the sharing of unsterilized hypodermic needles.

It would make a good study to investigate how many billions of dollars private citizens have been forced to pay in higher insurance fees for treatment of those with AIDS as a pre-existing condition, fees over and above the many billions government has spent directly on AIDS research and treatment.

Again, this regulation does not mention homosexuality or sexual orientation. But again, homosexual political activists take credit for bringing about regulations relating to AIDS. (See, for example, D'Emilio 1993, 70–71.) Why, of all diseases, do the California insurance regulations single out AIDS as a disease that must not be tested for? Clearly, the reason is that AIDS is a disease that afflicts homosexuals proportionally far more than heterosexuals. The homosexual activists want to obliterate the right of others—this time, insurance companies—to judge homosexuals based on the consequences of the homosexuals' actions.

Leading pro-homosexual political activist and historian John D'Emilio (1993, 76) writes admiringly of the following episode of homosexual activism:

> The network of sexual meeting places that fostered rec
> reational sex among gay men provided a hospitable

environment for the rapid spread of the virus, and the AIDS caseload grew exponentially. By 1987 there were more than forty-five thousand cases in the nation and more than forty-four hundred in San Francisco. The overwhelming majority of the San Francisco cases were among gay men.

...

Although AIDS was an unparalleled tragedy for the gay community around the nation, it also fostered a heightened level of political organizing. Wherever cases appeared in significant numbers, new organizations sprang to life to deal with the suffering. By the mid-1980s AIDS was pushing gay issues toward the center of public debate. Groups that formed to provide social services soon found it necessary to plunge into the political arena to demand more funding for research and support services, to lobby for protection against discrimination, and to ward off the Orwellian proposals of right-wing pressure groups. The March on Washington in October 1987, in which 600,000 gay men, lesbians, and their allies converged on the nation's capital, testified to the depth of anger and political militancy that the AIDS crisis had generated.

In this same article, D'Emilio (1993, 61) writes,

Capitalist society differentiates according to gender, class, and, race.

In other words, homosexuals engaged in barbaric practices which brought about a new epidemic—in addition to the prior, known epidemics of other venereal diseases they had fostered—then demanded money from other people to save them, forced these other people to have economic and social intercourse with them, and then—en masse—expressed their anger and *militancy* against the very people who had done so much to save them. And it's all the fault of capitalist society.

This article by D'Emilio appears in a college upper class and graduate school textbook on *psychology*. The book, *Psychological Perspectives on Lesbian & Gay Male Experiences* (Garnets & Kimmel, 1993), is an anthology (in its second edition as of 2015) of articles from leading researchers in the field. Here is a snippet from another article (Ratner 1993, 568) in the same textbook:

> Despite the different geographic areas and sampling methods used in the studies, it is clear that gay men and lesbians have more problems related to substance abuse than do heterosexuals. (McKirnan and Peterson 1989). Explanations for the phenomenon include internalization of society's homophobia [an alleged fear of homosexuals], nonacceptance of self, fear of coming out.

Numerous other articles referenced in this book, along with countless other books and articles on psychology and "gender studies," trumpet a similar line. The shared ideology is that there must be nothing wrong with homosexuality, that the problems experienced by homosexuals are caused by disapproving Western capitalist society and its "socially constructed" ideas such as "heterosexual masculinity" (a term used by Herek [1986] 1993) or "hegemonic masculinity and emphasized femininity" (terms used by Connell 1987, 183–190), that homosexuals need more than the protection of their individual rights: they need our "sick" society, consisting of too many sick heterosexuals—such as I, who took a twenty-five-question, multiple choice "psychological" test, anonymously over the Internet, that "diagnosed" me as "homophobic"—to be forced to accept and "affirm" homosexuals and prohibited from criticizing them. (Later, I will discuss these writings in more depth. See Frontline n.d. for the questionnaire on "homophobia." See Steyn 2013 regarding attempts by government to prohibit criticism of homosexuality.)

Academia and the psychological professions explicitly embrace this ideology—not to be questioned under penalty of professional censure (Gonsiorek 1991, 136)—in explaining away every affliction rampant among homosexuals, from depression and suicide to drug and alcohol abuse to promiscuity. (See, for example, Gonsiorek 1991, Gonsiorek and Rudolph 1991 for such explaining away of the statistically prevalent problems among homosexuals.)

By the argument that most of the self-destructive behavior by homosexuals is due to criticism from others, it would follow that most CEOs, TEA Partiers, political conservatives, and Objectivists (adherents of Ayn Rand's philosophy of Objectivism)—all of whom are routinely condemned and ridiculed by all the leading institutions of contemporary culture—would have committed suicide by now.

Garnets and Peplau (2001, 112), two leading psychologists in "gender studies," explain this explicit policy as follows:

> Today, therapists and their professional associations reject an "illness model" which suggested that heterosexuals are normal and mentally healthy, but homosexuals are abnormal and impaired in their psychological functioning (see review by Gonsiorek, 1991). Instead, an affirmative approach to practice has emerged that focuses on helping lesbians, gay men, and bisexuals to cope adaptively with the impact of stigma, minority status, and difference from the heterosexual mainstream (see the Guidelines for Psychotherapy with Lesbian, Gay, and Bisexual Clients that were adopted in 2000 by the American Psychological Association Council of Representatives).

This same policy is echoed and amplified, eight years later, by the American Psychological Association Task Force on Appropriate Therapeutic Responses to Sexual Orientation (2009, 11). The introduction to the 130-page report begins as follows:

In the mid-1970s, on the basis of emerging scientific evidence and encouraged by the social movement for ending sexual orientation discrimination, the American Psychological Association (APA) and other professional organizations affirmed that homosexuality per se is not a mental disorder and rejected the stigma of mental illness that the medical and mental health professions had previously placed on sexual minorities. This action, along with the earlier action of the American Psychiatric Association that removed *homosexuality* from the *Diagnostic and Statistical Manual of Mental Disorders* (*DSM*; American Psychiatric Association, 1973), helped counter the social stigma that the mental illness concept had helped to create and maintain. Through the 1970s and 1980s, APA and its peer organizations not only adopted a range of position statements supporting nondiscrimination on the basis of sexual orientation (APA, 1975, 2005a; American Psychiatric Association, 1973; American Psychoanalytic Association, 1991, 1992; National Association of Social Workers [NASW], 2003) but also acted on the basis of those positions to advocate for legal and policy changes (APA, 2003, 2005a, 2008b; NASW, 2003). On the basis of growing scientific evidence (Gonsiorek, 1991), licensed mental health providers (LMHP) of all professions increasingly took the perspective throughout this period that homosexuality per se is a normal variant of human sexuality and that lesbian, gay, and bisexual (LGB) people deserve to be affirmed and supported in their sexual orientation, relationships, and social opportunities. This approach to psychotherapy is generally termed *affirmative*, *gay affirmative*, or *lesbian, gay, and bisexual (LGB) affirmative*.

This alternative between "illness" and "affirmation" is a false alternative. For example, subjectivism or altruism or nihilism are not illnesses; they are wrong ideas. Though such ideas may lead to illness over time, the ideas per se are not illnesses. But that does not mean that such ideas should be "affirmed." Being a subjectivist, altruist, or nihilist is going to harm one's life.

It is not the province of psychology in particular to identify whether ideas such as altruism or nihilism are good or bad; such identifications are the province of philosophy. But there is something related to such ideas that psychology in particular must identify. Psychology must help an individual identify whether his explicit philosophical ideas are consistent with the philosophical ideas implicit in his daily psychological functioning. For instance, if the individual holds an explicit moral code of rational selfishness—which is contrary to altruism—psychology can help him identify whether he feels, in some situations, moral guilt consistent with an altruist premise. One objective standard for healthy psychological functioning is consistency between one's explicit ideas and one's subconsciously held premises. But such a standard is not one that the psychological professional considers in regard to sexual orientation, as we shall see.

Moreover, though it is philosophy that evaluates ideas such as altruism and nihilism, psychological professionals are not off the hook in having to take their own evaluative stand regarding such ideas. Ultimately, ideas such as subjectivism or altruism or nihilism cannot be practiced consistently, except in suicide. It takes knowledge of philosophy to know that fact. Every professional in every field needs a philosophy, and psychological professionals are no exception.

Note also the traces of political advocacy in the APA quotation above. Those traces are more overt in this passage later (p. 23) in the same report:

> In recognition of the legal nexus between psychiatric
> diagnosis and civil rights discrimination, especially for
> government employees, activists within the homophile

rights movement, including Frank Kameny and the
Mattachine Society of Washington, DC, launched a
campaign in late 1962 and early 1963 to remove homosexuality as a mental disorder from the American Psychiatric Association's *DSM* (D'Emilio, 1983; Kameny,
2009). This campaign grew stronger in the aftermath of
the Stonewall riots in 1969. Those riots were a water-
shed, as the movement for gay and lesbian civil rights
was embraced openly by thousands rather than limited
to small activist groups (D' Emilio, 1983; Katz, 1995).
In the area of mental health, given the results of research, activists within and outside of the professions
led a large and vocal advocacy effort directed at mental
health professional associations, such as the American
Psychiatric Association, the American Psychological
Association, and the American Association for Behavior Therapy, and called for the evaluation of prejudice
and stigma within mental health associations and practices (D'Emilio, 1983; Kameny, 2009).
...
Upon the recommendation of its committee evaluating
the research, the American Psychiatric Association
Board of Trustees and general membership voted to remove homosexuality per se from the DSM in December
1973 (Bayer, 1981). The American Psychiatric Association (1973) then issued a position statement supporting
civil rights protection for gay people in employment,
housing, public accommodation, and licensing, and the
repeal of all sodomy laws.

Keep in mind that this document is an official report from the
leading American professional organization of *psychologists*, not
avowed political Leftists.

The "large and vocal advocacy effort directed at mental health professional associations" consisted of standard New Leftist tactics of breaking into and disrupting private meetings, and stalking and harassing individuals—tactics that the perpetrators openly "affirm." This passage is from the transcript of a radio documentary by Alix Spiegel (2002), who gives the clear impression of being on the side of the homosexual activists:

> Alix Spiegel: This is Garry Allender, one of the gay activists who infiltrated the APA convention. He says that while one group of activists stormed a session on behavioral therapy, another combed the halls looking for [Irving] Bieber [one of the two leading psychiatrists opposed to the homosexual activist position]. They found him at a panel on transsexuals and homosexuality.

> Toby Bieber [Irving Bieber's wife]: And a group came storming in, dressed rather fantastically, with feathers in their hats as though they were going to attend to some costume ball. Making noise, and broke up the meeting. They broke it up.

> Garry Allender: We were not polite. We were not quiet. We were not asking for favors. We were just trying to delegitimize their authority and we felt they were oppressing us and here was finally a chance to talk back to them.

> Alix Spiegel: The protesters yelled at the psychiatrists. They called them sadists, they called them oppressors. But the protesters had an entirely different word for Irving Bieber. A word, which in the account that circulated after the event got a disproportionate amount of attention. To the protesters Dr. Bieber was not just your run of the mill sadist oppressor. No sir. Irving

Bieber was a mother[BLEEP].

...

[Alix Spiegel:] Personally, Bieber and [Charles] Socarides [the other leading psychiatrist opposed to the homosexual activist position] had become targets. Angry
gay activists followed them around, protesting every
paper. There were threatening phone calls late at night,
and obscene messages scratched into the paint of department bathroom stalls.

The fact that the American Psychiatric Association removed homosexuality as a mental disorder from its DSM in 1973—a decision
made by a *vote* of members, 5,854 to 3,810—is reported in article after article in the professional and popular literature on psychology.
These articles do not mention the threatening tactics, nor do they
mention the following passage in the actual published decision by
the American Psychiatric Association (1973, 2–3):

For a mental or psychiatric condition to be considered
a psychiatric disorder, it must either regularly cause
subjective distress, or regularly be associated with some
generalized impairment in social effectiveness or functioning.

...

If homosexuality per se does not meet the criteria for a
psychiatric disorder, what is it? Descriptively, it is one
form of sexual behavior. Our profession need not now
agree on its origin, significance, and value for human
happiness when we acknowledge that by itself it does
not meet the requirements for a psychiatric disorder.
Similarly, by no longer listing it as a psychiatric disorder we are not saying that it is "normal" or as valuable
as heterosexuality.

...

No doubt, homosexual activist groups will claim that
psychiatry has at last recognized that homosexuality is
as "normal" as heterosexuality. They will be wrong. In
removing homosexuality per se from the nomenclature
we are only recognizing that by itself homosexuality
does not meet the criteria for being considered a psychiatric disorder. We will in no way be aligning our-
selves with any particular viewpoint regarding the etiology or desirability of homosexual behavior.

The first paragraph above indicates the underlying subjectivism
of the standard of mental illness used by the American Psychiatric
Association in judging homosexuality. Illness in this case is considered a matter either of personal subjectivity ("subjective distress") or
social subjectivity ("social effectiveness or functioning"). There is no
mention of an objective standard, such as the one I mentioned above
regarding a comparison of a patient's implicit ideas to his explicit
ideas, even though psychiatrists do operate on that objective standard in many cases.

Socarides (1992), a Freudian, reports that the subjective standards named in the first paragraph quoted above were not the usual
standards actually applied in practice by psychiatrists to judge a psychiatric disorder. Socarides identifies the usual standard:

Psychoanalysts comprehend the meaning of a particular act of human behavior by delving into the motivational state from which it issues. ... When individuals
with similar behavior are analytically investigated, we
then arrive at objective conclusions as to the meaning
and significance of a particular phenomenon under examination.

It is a sad testament to the state of the professions of psychology
that the Freudians seem to be, relatively, the voices of reason and

objectivity. But see later. (For an analysis—a philosophical analysis—of Freud, see also Peikoff 1982, 211–214.)

Regarding the passage I quoted above from the American Psychiatric Association, the first sentence of the last paragraph proved prescient: "No doubt, homosexual activist groups will claim that psychiatry has at last recognized that homosexuality is as 'normal' as heterosexuality." It turns out, moreover, that the phrase "homosexual activist groups" subsumed mainstream academia, the psychological professions, and the mainstream press. The statement's qualification, "we are not saying that it is 'normal' or as valuable as heterosexuality," surprising in its reasonableness, has been ignored by all these groups.

Another important issue is the means by which each of the two sides in this debate measures psychological health or illness. On the side that homosexuality is not an illness, an article that is cited perhaps most often is Gonsiorek 1991. Since the publication of this article, which is a survey of other research, this side has considered the question closed. Indeed, Gonsiorek (1991) writes,

> The meticulous reader will note that much of the research reviewed here occurred in the 1960s and 1970s. ... This research was so consistent in its lack of findings suggesting inherent psychopathology in homosexuality that researchers began moving on to other projects by the 1980s. Recent research has dropped off because the question of inherent pathology in homosexuality has been answered from a scientific point of view and has not been seen as requiring more research.

Let us examine what Gonsiorek considers "scientific."

In the main part of his article, Gonsiorek (1991, 128–132) cites roughly two dozen studies that "directly addressed whether homosexuality per se is pathological." One group of them, which do argue for more psychopathology among homosexuals than heterosexuals,

Gonsiorek dismisses as flawed, and he goes into much detail about why he thinks they are flawed. Regarding the other group of studies, Gonsiorek simply cites them and names the psychological tests used, without describing any further the methods of the studies. Among these studies, most reported no difference between homosexuals and heterosexuals, and a few reported some difference. But regarding all the studies, including the ones Gonsiorek favors, he writes (1991, 128),

> The studies discussed below have sampling problems to various degrees ... .

One could read and scrutinize the studies that Gonsiorek finds favorable to his conclusion, but there really is no need to, because Gonsiorek tells us something else important about all of the studies he discusses in his article.

A few of the studies that Gonsiorek favors were based entirely on Rorschach tests, which ask subjects to describe what kinds of images they see in inkblot designs. The remaining studies, the vast majority of them, were based entirely on *multiple-choice tests*. Gonsiorek (1991, 131) writes,

> All of the studies reviewed so far have utilized objective personality measures, which use an objectively scored, usually true-false format, and have a considerable body of empirical research to guide interpretation of the tests.

In other words, none of these tests entailed an actual, personal examination of any of the subjects. The subjects just checked "true" or "false" or some other multiple-choice answer to questions that asked them about their behavior or feelings or opinions.

The penultimate, brief section (before "Conclusions") of Gonsiorek's article (1991, 132–135) is "Research on Rates of Psychiatric Problems." Some of the "research" in this section reports little difference between homosexuals and heterosexuals, but most of it reports more problems—such as suicide and drug abuse—for homosexuals. As usual for defenders of homosexuality, Gonsiorek attributes these problems to "external stressors" (p. 135) from a disapproving society. But in this section again, all of the "research" is based on "interview questions" (p. 132), a "psychiatric questionnaire" (p, 133), and similar methods of collecting data—all in a multiple-choice format.

In short, in this entire article, supposedly the definitive article proving that homosexuality is not an illness, there is not one reported instance of an actual professional actually examining the *thinking* of a person being "tested." There is not one instance of a human subject communicating his thinking or line of reasoning in his own words. There are only check marks on multiple-choice questionnaires and forms.

How could such an approach be possible? Gonsiorek (1991, 135) explains how in his conclusion:

> The studies reviewed and the findings in this chapter ought to be the touchstone of further theory and research in the study of homosexuality, because they represent the most carefully designed, reliable, valid, and objective measures of <u>adjustment</u> in the armamentarium of the <u>behavioral</u> sciences. [Underlined emphasis added.]

In other words, Gonsiorek evidently believes that there is no need to understand a subject's thinking, because psychology is not about thinking; it is about *adjustment* of *behavior*.

Consider this contrary opinion by Socarides (1992):

> Only in the consultation room, using the technique of introspective reporting and free association, protected by all the laws of medicine, psychology, and psychiatry, will an individual reveal the hidden (even from himself)

meaning and reasons behind his act. The meaning of a particular act or piece of behavior can only be decided on the basis of the motivational context from which it arises.

For example, if a man is not sexually attracted to women, it is important to find out *why*, as I know why I am not sexually attracted to men.

Reasons why, expressed uniquely by each individual, do not so easily fit into tabulated results that "behavioral scientists"—who themselves attempt to avoid any thinking—consider "scientific." As Ayn Rand (1972, 35) observed in an article about the work of the seminal behaviorist B. F. Skinner,

> Many psychologists are envious of the prestige—and the achievements—of the physical sciences, which they try not to emulate, but to imitate.

To see how inane the "scientific psychological tests" typically are, see the test I referenced earlier regarding "homophobia" (Frontline n.d.). This test, like all the other "psychological tests" I examined—including two of the tests most often cited by Gonsiorek 1991: the Eyesenck Personality Inventory (designed by a behaviorist) and the Sixteen Personality Factor Questionnaire (designed by a eugenicist!)—is inane because it asks about feelings, behaviors, and opinions without asking for *reasons*.

Having reviewed these ideas and methods from the mainstream of the psychological professions, we are now in a position to understand what accounts for the blatant false alternative between illness and "affirmation" in assessing homosexuality. The psychological professions are interested in feelings and behavior, and perhaps even conclusions; but they are not interested in *thinking*.

Moreover, *thinking* is the only mental process that is subject to *volition*. If one discards thinking, one also discards volition.

The false alternative of illness vs. affirmation is the result of the false premise that sexual orientation is not the result of thinking, that it is outside of an individual's choice or control, like the color of one's skin, and that therefore we must accept it like the color of one's skin.

Alas, the Freudian Socarides shares this view. He writes (1992),

> The homosexual has no choice as regards his or her sexual object. The condition is unconsciously determined …
>
> …
>
> The nuclear core of true homosexuality is never a conscious choice, an act of will; but rather it is determined from the earliest period of childhood …

Statistics indicating high frequencies of pathology among homosexuals are not the main issue. Many, many homosexuals are better than the LGBT (Lesbian, Gay, Bisexual, Transgender) political activists, and are not suicidal, or drug addicts, or promiscuous. A much more important issue is that decent, rights-respecting homosexuals are being told by a monolithic psychological establishment that they do not need to identify and understand their own implicit ideas underlying their sex-specific sexual values—because there are no such ideas. There are no explicit and implicit ideas to compare, according to all schools of psychology, because sexual orientation is not an expression of ideas.

To discover the source of *that* idea, we must examine the dominant theories on the etiology—the cause—of sexual orientation. That examination will reveal even deeper premises of the LGBT activists and the entire mainstream of the psychological and related professions.

As we shall see, the conclusion predominant in the psychological professions, that sexual orientation is not an expression of an individual's thinking, is nothing more than a deduction from the premise that *sexuality* is not an expression of an individual's thinking.

4. Etiology of Sexual Orientation: The Mainstream Theories

Chapter 2 argued that sex-specific sexual evaluation is volitional in the same way that other aspects of sexual attraction and romantic love—as well as a sense of life and all other kinds of emotional responses—are volitional. All of these emotional responses are automatic and non-volitional in the present, but they are based on past, conscious, volitional evaluations. Moreover, all of these responses can be understood and deepened by identifying the past evaluations and making them explicit and conscious once again in the present. This kind of understanding is an integration of reason and emotion. My argument, supported by extensive observation of myself and others, was an application of the writings of Ayn Rand regarding emotions and regarding sense of life and romantic love in particular.

In short, I concluded that the etiology of sex-specific sexual evaluation is volition. My conclusion is the opposite of the dominant, mainstream theories.

Historically, there have been two main theories of the etiology of sexual orientation. These theories are biological determinism and social determinism. These two theories have dominated the field of psychology not only pertaining to the etiology of sexual orientation, but also pertaining to the etiology of virtually every character trait and personality trait. In expositions of these two theories, the possibility of volition is either rejected summarily or—more usually—never explicitly considered, seemingly as though researchers did not have a choice about rejecting choice.

Over the past few decades, a third mainstream theory has emerged, eclipsing even the theories of biological and social determinism. This theory is "social constructionism," which claims that "sexual orientation" is merely a notion—with no basis in fact—that has been "constructed" somehow by society as a whole. Proponents of this theory, which now predominates in academic writing in psychology, either make no mention of volition, or they consider individual volition as completely subordinate to the forces of society as a whole.

In the field of psychology, the rejection or subordination of volition long predates the contemporary debates regarding sexual orientation. Consider the following quotation of Robert M. Frumkin (1961, 439) in the entry entitled "Sexual Freedom" in *The Encyclopedia of Sexual Behavior*; this encyclopedia was edited by the leading psychologist Albert Ellis along with Albert Abarbanel, and published when virtually all psychological professionals still considered homosexuality a mental illness.

> The most distinctive characteristic of man as compared to non-human animals is that man's behavior is essentially learned, it is not innate or biologically determined. Thus, man's behavior is a social psychological phenomenon. And so is his sexual behavior.
>
> ...
>
> The nature of sexual behavior in man, like *all* his truly human behavior, varies with his culture, with reference to <u>the society in which he is socialized</u> and in which <u>he becomes a human, social being</u>. [Underlined emphasis added.]

> Freedom in popular usage is a term of little scientific precision. From the modern behavioral scientist's point of view, there is, in reality, no such thing as freedom as the word is generally used in everyday language. That is, the idea that every person has an ability, freedom, to act in accordance with his own inner conviction,

independent of the situation-process in which he is operating, is a fiction. The idea of free will, a concept closely related to the idea of freedom, must also be rejected. It too is fictitious.

This is the philosophical and psychological context—the "society in which" psychological professionals were "socialized"—that most psychological professionals have *chosen* to accept as a starting point in the debate over sexual orientation. Indeed, most psychological professionals have chosen this starting point regarding the entire subject of sexuality and the entire subject of psychology.

Note the last underlined phrase in the above passage from Frumkin. As we shall see later, social constructionists take this idea literally: that an individual is *not human* until he is *socialized*.

The following is the entire answer to the question, "What causes a person to have a particular sexual orientation?" in a brochure—intended for the general public—by the American Psychological Association (2008, 2):

> There is no consensus among scientists about the exact reasons that an individual develops a heterosexual, bisexual, gay, or lesbian orientation. Although much research has examined the possible genetic, hormonal, developmental, social, and cultural influences on sexual orientation, no findings have emerged that permit scientists to conclude that sexual orientation is determined by any particular factor or factors. Many think that nature and nurture both play complex roles; most people experience little or no sense of choice about their sexual orientation. [Underlined emphasis added.]

As we see, the American Psychological Association does not even consider volition as a possible cause of sexual orientation. And as we shall see, proponents of the two main traditional theories—"nature" and "nurture"—generally are very critical of each other's theory; and they arrive at their own theory by a process of elimination.

Of the two main traditional theories—"nature" and "nurture"— the *less* popular one among professionals in psychology is "nature," that is, biological determinism. Let us examine that theory first.

The term "biological determinism" does not exaggerate the position of this side of the debate. J. Michael Bailey (2003, 51–52), one of the leading biological researchers on sexual orientation, writes,

> The argument over whether homosexuality is biological or "freely chosen" is perhaps the most common and least productive version of the biology debate.
>
> ...
>
> Most scientists are both (strict) determinists and materialists. Determinism, in its strict sense, implies that all present events (including mental states and behaviors) are completely caused by past events. Equivalently, given a configuration of events at Time A, there can be exactly one configuration of events at later Time B. Materialists believe that all causes and effects obtain in the material world, as opposed to a nonmaterial "soul." Thus a materialist determinist acquainted with modern neuroscience believes (as I do) that all behavior is most proximately caused by brain states, and thus behavioral differences must be caused by brain differences. This is true even for socially acquired traits.

Thus the argument that biology determines sexual orientation is fundamentally a philosophical argument, not a scientific one, and the philosophy is wrong. The argument regarding sexual orientation is a mere deduction from the more general doctrine of biological determinism, the doctrine that biology determines *all* behavior. As a doctrine of determinism, biological determinism is self-refuting: if the doctrine were true, no one could know it (or anything else, for that matter), because believing the doctrine would be determined. More fundamentally, determinism contradicts one's direct awareness of one's own volition, an awareness as direct as one's awareness of material things. But let us see specifically how the wrong philosophy infects the "scientific reasoning" used by the biological determinists in their research.

Another main proponent of biological determinism is neuroscientist Simon LeVay. LeVay is well-known for a study (LeVay 1991) in which he reported a difference between heterosexual and homosexual men regarding the size of a particular part of the brain.

LeVay's book *Gay, Straight and the Reason Why* (2011), published by the prestigious Oxford University Press, is a comprehensive presentation of the evidence that sexual orientation is determined by biology. LeVay cites hundreds of studies regarding animals, genes, sex hormones, brain structure and function, body parts (such as ratios of finger length), and "birth order" (how many older brothers a child had).

The general pattern of many of the studies is as follows. The researchers take some measurement that seems to differ between men and women, such as the ratio of trunk (torso) length to limb length. (LeVay 2011, 224–227). Then they claim that homosexual men have an average measurement that is slightly skewed toward the women's average measurement. Then they also hypothesize some reason that the homosexual men had genes or pre-natal hormones that would cause both the skewed measurement and the same-sex sexual orientation. But various studies differ on the results, and some studies do not support the conclusions at all. (Note that LeVay does not claim that homosexual adults have levels of hormones—such as testosterone—that differ from the levels in heterosexual adults; LeVay claims instead that homosexuals had different levels of these hormones in the womb, causing these individuals to develop differently.)

Then there are studies that ask adults what their sexual orientation is, and what other physical and personality traits these individuals had as children. These studies affirm the existence of "gendered traits" (LeVay 2011, 74): traits that tend to differ between boys and girls, or between men and women.

LeVay (2011, 99) writes,

> In the area of personality, men rank higher than women on measures of assertiveness, competitiveness, aggressiveness, and <u>independence</u>. (These getting-things-done traits are sometimes referred to collectively as <u>instrumentality</u>.) Women rank higher than men on measures of expressiveness, sociability, empathy, openness to feelings, <u>altruism</u>, and <u>neuroticism</u>. (This last item includes the tendency to depression, anxiety, self-consciousness, and low self-esteem.) [Underlined emphasis added.]

LeVay (2011, 100) also writes,

> Men focus more than women on the youthfulness of their potential partners, whereas women focus more than men on nonphysical attributes such as personality, <u>wealth</u>, and <u>power</u>. [Underlined emphasis added.]

LeVay (2011, 101) concludes,

> As with childhood traits, the gendered traits of adults appear to be influenced by biological factors, such as genes and sex hormones. First, many of the sex differences exist widely across different countries and cultures, including illiterate populations as well as those that are more egalitarian. In fact, contrary to what one might expect on the basis of a simple socialization model, gender differences in personality seem to

become more marked as societies cast off traditional
expectations about the roles of men and women.

In other words, LeVay argues that because these "gendered traits"
are not caused by society, they must be caused by biology. Thus
LeVay is arguing that biology determines much more than sexual
orientation. He is arguing that biology determines ideas and/or practices related to ethics: such ideas and/or practices as "independence"
and "altruism," explicitly named by LeVay. He is also arguing that
biology causes some women to be attracted to wealth, a trait that one
might accurately describe as being a "gold digger."

This theory is a doctrine of innate ideas and therefore should be
dismissed out-of-hand on philosophical grounds. Either this doctrine presumes the existence of ideas without any perceptual
knowledge to underlie them—that is, this doctrine is a form of mys-
ticism—or this doctrine denies that what we generally think of as
ideas are ideas at all, and thus this doctrine is a form of materialism.

LeVay (2011, 119–125) then cites studies claiming that the measurements of these "gendered traits" in homosexuals are somewhat
skewed toward the gender opposite to their own. That is, homosexual men are somewhat altruistic gold-diggers like heterosexual
women, and lesbians are somewhat aggressive competitors like heterosexual men. From this evidence, LeVay concludes that sexual orientation too must be biologically determined.

In other words, LeVay's claim that sexual orientation is biologically determined is a deduction from the premise that a whole constellation of character traits and personality traits—including *ideas*
and *values*—is biologically determined.

Ironically, LeVay's argument (2011, 119–125) that biology causes
sexual orientation has even less empirical data than his argument
that biology causes ideas such as altruism and gold-digger-ism: homosexuals exhibit these "gendered traits" only partly skewed toward
the sex opposite to their own.

One more variant of LeVay's basic argument is worth mentioning. The data that LeVay (2011, 247–270) cites that have the most dramatic numerical measurements pertain to some studies regarding "the older-brother effect." According to this notion, a male child is more likely to become homosexual if he has an older brother. The theory is that having an older brother causes the younger brother to be exposed to less testosterone in the womb. (Again, LeVay's point is not that these individuals have less than normal male levels of testosterone when they are adults, but only while they are developing in the womb.) LeVay notes (2011, 251–255) that several very large studies contradict the studies that he favors, but he persists:

> My take on the entire collection of studies is that gay men do have significantly more older brothers, on average, than straight men. If this were not the case, some systematic error would have to have biased the Canadians' many studies and the positive findings of several other researchers. No one has been able to pinpoint such an error. That some studies have failed to detect an older brother effect may result from methodological issues, atypical samples, or pure chance. (Blanchard has spelled out what he considers the weaknesses of some of the negative studies.)

In other words, no one has pinpointed errors in either the positive or negative studies, but when errors are found, they may be in the negative studies.

A good summary of much of the book's whole approach is given inadvertently by LeVay (2011, 183) in a footnote describing a particular study:

> This by way of demonstrating that, with sufficient ingenuity, any inconvenient finding can be explained away.

But I have not yet come to the main point regarding these older-brother studies. According to the most positive studies, the probability of a boy being homosexual goes up, if he has one brother, from 2% to nearly 3%; if he has two brothers, the probability goes up to nearly 4%. From this change of one or two per cent, LeVay concludes that sexual orientation is 100% caused by biology. How does he draw this conclusion?

He draws this conclusion by a process of elimination. He gives some arguments (LeVay 2011, 267–270) that the older-brother effect cannot be based on environment. He then concludes (LeVay, 2011, 285) that the only causal factor must be biology: there must be some boundary amount of testosterone whereby, if a male fetus gets less than this amount, it definitely becomes homosexual; and if the male fetus gets more than this amount, it definitely becomes heterosexual.

And now we come to the main premise that makes this entire argument possible: LeVay rejects, at the beginning of his book (2011), the possibility of volition.

LeVay's book has nearly 300 pages of text; but only two of those pages are devoted to the question of volition. The book has 561 reference notes; but only three of these notes are on the question of volition. The four cited references (LeVay 2012, 41) in these three notes are the *Los Angeles Times* daily newspaper regarding a *Los Angeles Times* poll, *The New York Times* regarding a poll of opinions about homosexuality, and two analyses by the RAND Institute of "the responses of gay men and lesbians to a questionnaire in *The Advocate*, a leading gay magazine." From this evidence, LeVay (2011, 41) concludes categorically,

> If their sexual orientation was indeed a choice, gay people should remember having made it. But, by and large, they don't.

As explained in Chapter 2, however, people generally do not remember choosing *any* aspect of their sense of life. Nor do they remember choosing to respond emotionally to certain styles of art. Nor do they remember choosing to respond sexually (or to be averse sexually) to intelligence, ability, moral virtue, power, wealth, violence, etc.

If any of the statistical correlations reported by LeVay are accurate, then there is a simple causal explanation—based on volition—for such correlations. If a boy is born with less testosterone and/or less-developed male physical traits, he may choose less physically vigorous activities, and he may even have lessened physical abilities. For such a boy or man, the choice to be heterosexual requires an extra amount of courage or knowledge, and some boys or men will not choose to exhibit that courage or seek that knowledge. But such correlations are only statistics. Physically strong boys can still make choices leading them away from heterosexuality, and physically weaker boys can still makes choice leading them to heterosexuality.

The entire argument of LeVay's book (2011) can be summarized as follows: LeVay eliminates volition—because of wrong philosophy and inadequate scholarship—at the outset, and then he eliminates environment in the various studies cited throughout the book; LeVay thereby arrives, by this process of elimination, at biology as the cause of sexual orientation. In truth, LeVay's argument for biological determinism of sexual orientation—along with the hundreds of studies LeVay cites—is worthless.

LeVay's book has some merits, though minor. LeVay (2011, 28–33) offers a good summary of Freudian theories of the etiology of sexual orientation, and he points out (in effect) that these theories violate Occam's Razor: they are very complex and implausible, without evidence in support of these complex theories. LeVay also identifies instances in which theories of social determinism are contradicted by empirical evidence. (See, for example, LeVay 2011, 33–40). In his arguments, however, LeVay does not identify the main refutation of these other theories, that refutation being volition.

The materialism underlying LeVay's approach integrates with the statements, quoted earlier, by Bailey. Indeed, LeVay cites fourteen different studies by Bailey. LeVay's (2011, 15) favorable description of some of these studies provides further perspective on the mindset of biological determinists studying sexual orientation:

> Michael Bailey and his colleagues at Northwestern University ... have studied the sexual orientation of both men and women by measuring genital arousal during the viewing of erotic videos.

Presumably, a man not sexually aroused by watching strange women perform sex acts is not a true heterosexual; and a man who is aroused by such women would be considered healthy if he had sex with all of them.

These researchers have no conception of sexual attraction as a response to values—*any* values, not just a person's sex. To these people, sexuality is mindless. They are sexual nihilists. It is no wonder that they conclude that sexual orientation is mindless.

Unlike the arch materialist-determinist Bailey, LeVay at least offers some empirical argument—of sorts—against volition; LeVay at least devotes two pages to considering volition. That is two pages more than what the other mainstream side of this debate considers.

Since the publication of the first edition of the present book, even more evidence has appeared against the theory that sexual orientation is biologically determined. In a highly publicized study appearing in *Science*, Ganna et al. (2019, eaat7694) "performed a genome-wide association study (GWAS) on 477,522 individuals," and concluded that "all tested genetic variants ... do not allow meaningful prediction of an individual's sexual behavior." Mayer and McHugh 2016 and Diamond and Rosky 2016, both systematic reviews of past research, both report that sexual orientation has been observed to be highly fluid over time in many individuals. Not surprisingly, the fluidity is usually in the direction of heterosexuality. (Mayer and

McHugh 2016 also reports that "gender dysphoria" in children usually subsides.)

Although the notion that biology determines sexual orientation is popular in the popular press and among non-academic LGBT activists, the notion is a minority opinion among academic writers and psychological professionals. For example, the "historian" D'Emilio (2009), often cited by mainstream psychologists (as in the instances I mentioned in Chapter 3), stated in a friendly interview with the *International Socialist Review*,

> The idea that people are born gay—or lesbian or bisexual—is appealing for lots of reasons. Many of us experience the direction of our sexual desires as something that we have no control over. We just are that way, it seems, so therefore we must be born gay. The people who are most overt in their hatred of queer folks, the religious conservatives, insist that being gay is something we choose, and we know we can't agree with them. Hence, again, born gay. ...
>
> "Born gay" is an idea with a large constituency, LGBT and otherwise. It's an idea designed to allay the ingrained fears of a homophobic society and the internalized fears of gays, lesbians, and bisexuals. <u>What's most amazing to me about the "born gay" phenomenon is that the scientific evidence for it is thin as a reed</u>, yet it doesn't matter. It's an idea with such <u>social utility</u> that one doesn't need much evidence in order to make it attractive and credible. [Underlined emphasis added.]

Note also the philosophical Pragmatism in D'Emilio's comment. According to D'Emilio, an idea—though false—yet has "social utility." Presumably, there then must be "social utility" in outright lying about history—D'Emilio is a "historian"—or science or anything else. This mentality illustrates that political Leftists generally consider dishonesty a legitimate and important tactic in achieving their goals.

Diamond and Rosky 2016, published soon after the *Obergefell* decision by the United States Supreme Court made it illegal for U.S. states to restrict same-sex marriage, is another illustration of lying as a Leftist political tactic. Diamond and Rosky were staunch LGBT advocates highly regarded by the LGBT movement. The abstract of their article begins as follows:

> We review scientific research and legal authorities to argue that the immutability of sexual orientation should no longer be invoked as a foundation for the rights of individuals with same-sex attractions and relationships (i.e., sexual minorities). On the basis of scientific research as well as U.S. legal rulings regarding lesbian, gay, and bisexual (LGB) rights, we make three claims: First, arguments based on the immutability of sexual orientation are unscientific, given what we now know from longitudinal, population-based studies of naturally occurring changes in the same-sex attractions of some individuals over time. Second, arguments based on the immutability of sexual orientation are unnecessary, in light of U.S. legal decisions in which courts have used grounds other than immutability to protect the rights of sexual minorities.

What do the authors mean by the curious statement, "arguments based on the immutability of sexual orientation are unnecessary"? If the arguments are wrong, what does it mean to add the statement that the arguments are unnecessary? Are some wrong arguments necessary?

The meaning of this curious statement becomes clearer from the following text from the body of the article (Diamond and Rosky 2016, 372–373):

the perception that immutability claims are fundamentally linked to sexual-minority civil rights is so pervasive that public figures who question immutability arguments are reflexively considered homophobic [references]. Scientists themselves (including the first author) have sometimes contributed to misconceptions about the immutability of sexual orientation by failing to challenge and unpack these misconceptions in the media, often to avoid having their statements misused by antigay activists [references]. …

When immutability claims are the only way to save lives, it makes both strategic and moral sense for scientists and advocates to highlight scientific findings that support these claims. Yet in the United States, the social and legal context is obviously more favorable to sexual-minority rights, and immutability claims are no longer necessary, nor particularly effective. …

This is not to say that these claims have no utility whatsoever. For sexual minorities who do experience their same-sex sexuality as early-developing and unchanging, immutability arguments may resonate with their experiences and provide them with a meaningful foundation for their self-acceptance. Also, within highly rejecting contexts (such as a family threatening to disown a gay child because they view same-sex sexuality as a moral failing), immutability arguments may reduce rejection and stigma by countering the view of same-sex sexuality as "blameworthy."

In short, lying—including lying by one of the authors—has been useful in the past; but lying is "no longer necessary"—though still useful in some cases.

As the argument for biological determinism is largely an argument by process of elimination, so too is the argument for social determinism. Social determinists consider volition little or not at all; then they undermine the case for biological determinism; and then they deduce that the only cause of sexual orientation must be society. Or sometimes they argue that biology has *some* causal effect, but society too has a large effect.

More specifically, the common academic arguments against biological determinism of sexual orientation are as follows:

1. The studies in favor of biological determinism are countered by other studies that do not replicate the favorable results; moreover, even the studies in favor are flawed. (See, for example, Peplau et al. 1999, 75–81; Jones 2012, 6–12.)

2. Social determinists argue that sexual orientation is variable and changeable. Common sexual orientations vary from culture to culture; many individuals change their sexual orientation over the course of their life (as argued above by Diamond and Rosky 2016); and some primitive tribes even prescribe a series of changing stages of sexual orientation for every individual in the tribe.

This second argument, though useless as an argument against volition, is in my judgment a strong argument against biological determinism. Interestingly, even social determinists generally admit that they do not understand how society or environment determines sexual orientation; but they deduce that it must be so, because the cause must not be biology. For example, Peplau et al. (1999, 80) write,

> Currently, proponents of genetic perspectives view the research evidence as encouraging and justifying the search for specific genetic markers of sexual orientation. In contrast, skeptics emphasize possible limitations of available studies (e.g., McGuire, 1995). These include the inability of current research to <u>disentangle the impact of genes and environment</u> on family

members' sexual orientation ... [Underlined emphasis added.]

Neither Peplau nor other leading psychologists seem to think there is a need to "disentangle the impact" of *volition* from "genes and environment." Therefore, once they eliminate biology as a possible cause, Peplau et al. (1999, 87) can conclude,

> cross-cultural and historical analyses demonstrate that women's erotic and romantic bonds can take diverse forms that are shaped by their social environment.

Of course, a doctrine of social determinism, like biological determinism, contradicts our direct knowledge of volition. But to get a sense of the kind of thinking involved in the argument for social determinism, consider the following quotations.

Peplau (2001, 11) writes,

> Also relevant is evidence that female primate sexual behavior varies as a function of the social context. For example, when rhesus monkeys are housed in male-female pairs, mating occurs throughout the female's cycle. In contrast, when rhesus monkeys live in larger social groups, mating is generally restricted to the female's period of fertility. Wallen (1995) explained this shift as resulting from the social structure and interaction patterns that emerge in larger groups.

The fact that Peplau, a leading academic psychologist cited favorably in the ruling by the U.S. District Court overturning California's Proposition 8 (a proposition stating that "only marriage between a man and a woman is valid or recognized in California"), cites the behavior of animals to make her point reveals her attitude toward volition.

In the same article, Peplau (2001, 3) writes,

in a region of southern Africa it was common for adolescent schoolgirls to engage in a form of institutionalized friendship known as "mummy-baby relations" (Gay, 1986). In this arrangement, an older girl (the "mummy" or mother) formed an emotionally close relationship with a younger girl (the "baby"). The girls exchanged love letters, and the older girl provided gifts and advice about becoming a woman. The most important aspect of mummy-baby friendship was the expression of affection and intimacy. These relationships sometimes but not always had a genital sex component. The mummy-baby relationship allowed teen-age girls to learn about their developing sexuality without fear of pregnancy and in a context condoned by parents and teachers.

Later, Peplau (2001, 4) writes,

In rural Lesotho in Africa, prior to Western influences, it was common for married women to have a special, long-term female friend or motsoalle (Kendall, 1999). These loving sexual relationships were celebrated with a ritual feast in which the entire community acknowledged the commitment that the two women were making to each other.

In these and numerous other cases in this article, Peplau gives the distinct impression that she approves of all these social-sexual relationships involving children and multiple concurrent sex partners. (The only kind of arrangement that she cites disapprovingly is the custom of arranged heterosexual marriages in nineteenth-century China.) As we have already seen, and as we will continue to see, this kind of amoral "affirmation" of homosexuality—not to mention pedophilia—is the rule, not the exception, in the psychological professions today.

In rejecting the notion that biology causes sexual orientation, Peplau ends up endorsing an even more basic role for biology. Peplau (2001, 14) writes favorably of an

> analysis provided by Helen Fisher (1998), who emphasized the possible neuroendocrine underpinnings for adult romantic relationships. Fisher distinguished among <u>three major emotional systems that guide mammalian mating</u>. The sex drive, associated primarily with estrogen and androgens, motivates individuals to seek sex with other members of their species but does not focus on a particular partner. Attraction, also called infatuation or passionate love in humans, is characterized by focused attention on a specific partner, increased energy and, in humans, with feelings of exhilaration and preoccupation. Research links this system with the catecholamines (e.g., dopamine and norepinephrine) and also with serotonin and phenylethylamine. The third system is attachment, characterized by close social contact and, in humans, by feelings of calm, comfort, and emotional bonding. There is considerable evidence that attachment is associated with oxytocin and vasopressin. ...
>
> Although sexual desire, infatuation/attraction, and attachment are distinct processes, <u>they are not entirely unrelated</u>. Neuroscience offers hints about their <u>possible</u> interconnections. (Underlined emphasis added.]

It is nice to know that contemporary psychologists think that sexual desire and romantic love are not *entirely* unrelated. Unfortunately, these psychologists believe that the relation is *hormonal*. Peplau continues that these "three major emotional systems that guide mammalian mating"—"sex drive," "infatuation/attraction," and "attachment"—are more interconnected hormonally in women than in men, thereby explaining why women connect sex and "attachment" more than men do. (I suppose men are out of luck.) Peplau (2001, 15) then concludes that this connection

> may help to explain a puzzling aspect of women's same-sex relationships—how an emotionally intense friendship can kindle sexual desire.

In other words, the one aspect of a sexual relationship that Peplau thinks needs explaining is how two people can be attracted to each other for non-physical reasons. She solves the problem by arguing that the cause is physical—in this case, hormonal—after all.

Observe this irony. The biological determinists argue that biology causes sexual orientation because biology causes everything. The social determinists end up arguing that biology does *not* cause sexual orientation, because biology causes everything *else* about sexual desire and romantic "attachment"; but society causes, in part, sexual orientation.

In Chapter 2, I described how a person processes, through acts of volition, his experiences. Those who claim that "social and cultural influences" determine sexual orientation refer to these same experiences. Social determinists claim that the experiences themselves determine sexual orientation. But we know that our conscious mind is available to witness all our experiences—otherwise they would not be experiences—and along with being the witness, we are also the judge and jury regarding these experiences. It is our own verdicts on each experience that cause our emotions.

In short, every argument against biological determinism by the social determinists or social constructionists is, when revised to correct its philosophical error, an argument in favor of free will.

Most of these researchers ultimately admit that they really do not know the etiology of sexual orientation. Recall the statement, which I quoted earlier, by the American Psychological Association (2008, 2):

> Although much research has examined the possible ge-
> netic, hormonal, developmental, social, and cultural in-
> fluences on sexual orientation, no findings have
> emerged that permit scientists to conclude that sexual
> orientation is determined by any particular factor or
> factors.

So long as these "scientists" deny volition, they never will find the answer.

Indeed, many researchers seem to have stopped trying to find an answer. Their new approach is to try to make the question go away. This approach should be familiar to students of the history of philosophy; the approach has been used by Kant regarding the question of knowledge of reality, by positivists regarding questions of metaphysics, and by contemporary philosophy regarding knowledge, reason, ethics, and philosophy itself. As we shall see, the psychological professions have relied heavily on this philosophical tradition.

Among psychologists, the new dominant school of thought regarding sexual orientation is "social constructionism." (Peplau is a social constructionist.) All of the social constructionists that I have read dwell on the same themes, as if their "ideas" were "socially constructed" by modern psychology rather than having been reached individually through a process of reason. Let us consider two articles by one of the most prominent social constructionists regarding sexual orientation: Gregory M. Herek, who has been involved professionally in numerous U.S. and state Supreme Court cases regarding sexual orientation.

Herek's entry, entitled "Homosexuality", in the *Encyclopedia of Psychology* published jointly by the American Psychological Association and Oxford University Press, states (2000, 151–152),

> Debate about the roots of sexual orientation has pitted
> those who consider it to be a universal human charac-
> teristic (some have also extended the concept to other

species) against those who regard all aspects of human
sexuality as socially constructed within a particular cultural context. [Underlined emphasis added.]

The sentence above contains a revealing word: "all." According
to Herek, it is not merely sexual orientation but rather "all aspects of
human sexuality" that are socially constructed.

But there are other important aspects to this statement that are
made clearer as Herek continues,

Proponents of the former viewpoint have hypothesized
biological (e.g., genetic and hormonal factors, the intra-
uterine environment of the developing fetus) or environmental (infant-caretaker interactions, learning, social interactions over the life span) determinants of sexual orientation. Social constructionists, in contrast,
have argued that although people engage in homosexual and heterosexual acts in all societies, such behavior
does not necessarily endow an individual with an identity or social role that corresponds to modern Western
notions of "heterosexuality" and "homosexuality."

There is a big changing of the subject that is going on here. Instead of pitting nature and nurture—that is, biological determinism
and environmental determinism—on opposite sides of the debate,
Herek is placing those two forms of determinism on the same one
side of the debate. Such a policy would be admirable if on the other
side he placed volition. But on the other side, he places the proposition that *there really is no such objective fact as sexual orientation.*

One can already see from these two snippets from Herek that this
notion of social construction is a form of nominalism, a denial that
any kind of conceptual identification could be based on objective
fact. But before analyzing the meaning of Herek's framing of the debate, let us examine another article, one in which Herek elaborates
on his own position as a social constructionist.

Herek ([1986] 1993), in an article cited hundreds of times in the professional literature (according to Google Scholar), briefly describes his view on the etiology of sexual orientation:

> Here we can make use of Freud's (1961 [1905]) assumption that humans are born with an amorphous, unformed sexuality—we are polymorphously perverse. Our behavioral repertoire is ambisexual. Over the course of individual development, the principal source of sexual arousal becomes located in the genitals for most people, and they find that they are aroused by a relatively limited range of things in the world—typically by human beings of a particular gender with fairly specific physical and psychological qualities. In other words, people acquire preferences for certain sexual partners, acts, and situations. Obviously, people are attracted to each other for a host of reasons other than gender—for example, physical appearance, intellect, personality, sense of humor, and religious and political affiliation. But gender is a basic consideration for most people, whether or not it is conscious. [Underlined emphasis added.]

Thus Herek, like LeVay, treats the etiology of sexual orientation the same way that he treats the etiology of attraction to fundamental character traits, personality traits, and value systems. Do all of these aspects of attraction occur without volition, as Herek suggests by the phrases "they find that they are aroused" and "acquire preferences"? Do all of these ideas—about intellect, religion, and politics—somehow get deposited in our brains without our ever having been conscious of them and having had an opportunity to judge them rationally? Such a position is a doctrine of social determinism, which—as I have already stated—is in contradiction to our direct knowledge of volition.

Moreover, are all of these aspects of attraction to be "affirmed" by psychologists, as sexual orientation is currently affirmed by psychologists, without scrutiny of the underlying ideas and judgments involved? Such a position would be absurd, as is the position to affirm every sexual orientation without scrutiny of the underlying ideas and judgments involved.

Herek does not answer such questions. His thesis addresses another matter altogether. He writes, ([1986] 1993, 322),

> There is an important difference between the words *heterosexual* and *homosexual* when they are used as adjectives, describing sexual behavior of which anyone is capable, and when they are used as nouns, describing identity.
>
> ...
>
> In many New Guinea societies, for example, becoming a man requires incorporating the semen of other men into one's own body through homosexual acts. Once manhood is achieved, heterosexual behavior is socially prescribed ... . [Here Herek cites references for these ridiculously irrelevant anthropological claims.] In some indigenous American societies, biological males could assume women's occupations and be recognized socially as women; some men in this "berdache" role married (biological and social) males. In some tribes, a comparable role was available to biological females ... .[Here he cites additional ridiculous references.]
>
> Such cross-cultural comparisons show that our notions of heterosexuals and homosexuals are part of a particular historically derived knowledge system. As socio-erotic identities, homosexuality and heterosexuality have been created within our culture, starting from the raw material of humans' inherent ambisexuality and

inevitable development of erotic and affectional preferences.

This is not to minimize the reality of homosexual or
heterosexual identities or to claim that they are simply
figments of our imagination that can be easily dismissed. Culturally constructed identities are not easily
changed. But it is important to realize that "heterosexuals" and "homosexuals" do not exist in nature; they are
constructs ... .

Observe that Herek is not referring to these backward tribes in
order to disprove biological determinism. He is citing them to try to
disprove the validity of our advanced society's concepts of sexual orientation.

Herek is claiming that heterosexuals and homosexuals are real
only in the sense of being notions that people really hold in their
mind, not in the sense of being actual individuals in reality.

Those who have not studied the history of philosophy might
think that Herek's argument is specific to the subject of sexual orientation. But the argument is a standard, centuries-old attack against
all conceptual knowledge.

For example, we could replace the words "heterosexual" and "homosexual" in Herek's argument with the words "honest" and "dishonest." Some men sometimes tell the truth and sometimes lie; these
men do not easily fit into the descriptions "honest man" or "dishonest man." Perhaps all the men in some tribe of cavemen sometimes
told the truth and sometimes lied. Therefore, by Herek's argument,
honest men and dishonest men do not exist in nature; they are constructs.

The same could be stated for words such as "good" and "bad";
"right" and "wrong"; "intelligent" and "dull"; "master," "slave," and
"free man"; "baker," "tailor," "pickpocket," and "psychologist"; even

"blue" and "green" (because some things are bluish green or part blue and part green).

Herek states above "that our notions of heterosexuals and homosexuals are part of a particular historically derived knowledge system." But what concepts are *not* part of a "historically derived knowledge system"? No concepts beyond very simple ones such as "dog" and "cat" could fit that bill.

The centuries-old argument that Herek is invoking begins with the nominalism of Hume, which holds that the forming of all concepts is arbitrary and can go along any equally non-objective path. Kant accepted Hume's attack on objectivity, but then added that there is a specific subjective path set by innate structures within each individual mind. Hegel, accepting the subjectivism of Kant but adding a twist, held that the path is set instead by a collective of minds.

Since Hume ([1777] 1902), nominalism has been a dominant theory of conceptualization in Western Philosophy. The Hume-Kant-Hegel line of thought has continued through Marxism, Nazism, and the Frankfurt School, and has these days been made fashionable in the form of postmodernism and so-called "Critical Theory." Because this Humean-Kantian-Hegelian argument could not get off the ground without nominalism, let us address that idea.

In the history of philosophy, the argument for nominalism consists of nothing more than a refutation of a straw man. The straw man is the philosophical notion that all entities contain reified essences—such as "blueness" or "homosexualness"—which we allegedly sense directly and infallibly, analogous to our sensing of light or sound, and which we use as the basis of our concepts. Nominalism's answer to this straw man is that there are no such essences and that therefore all concepts are mere naming conventions—hence the word "nominalism"—which have no basis in fact.

Using the terminology of Ayn Rand, Herek's nominalist position implies that if an idea is not intrinsic—that is, if the idea is not "intrinsic in reality, apart from any relation to man or his mind"

(Peikoff 1991, 142)—then the idea must be subjective, that is, "constructed" by some mind or group of minds without adherence to the facts of reality.

Conceptual, objective knowledge is not based on the intuiting of reified essences, but on the perception and identification of existents as falling within certain ranges of measurement as compared to other existents falling outside those ranges. For example, a five-foot-long stick and six-foot-long stick can be classified as "walking sticks" because they fall within a relatively narrow range of measurement of length within a broader spectrum of lengths of various sticks (such as twenty-foot-long sticks and one-foot-long sticks), that narrow range of measurement recognizing the sticks as suitable to aiding a man in walking. By Herek's nominalism, "walking sticks" do not exist in nature (even if they are branches that just fell off trees), but are rather subjective constructs. In truth, the conception "walking stick" is objective, furthering an understanding of reality—not a mere subjective whimsy projected onto reality—through and in terms of reality's real effects on man. The conception also leads to a practical benefit.

Similarly, a heterosexual is someone attracted enough to individuals of the opposite sex as to have a reasonable chance of mating with one of them, while having little or no such attraction to anyone of the same sex. Along with classifying myself as a heterosexual man, classifying certain individuals as heterosexual women enables me to identify them as possible candidates for romance, enhancing my chances of finding a mate. Most importantly, such a classification is a starting point for me to understand my sexual orientation, to make judgments about it, and to experience its benefits more fully. Indeed, this entire book is in pursuit of such understanding, judgments, and benefits. The concept "heterosexual" is objective, furthering an understanding of reality. The concept also leads to practical benefits. These benefits accrue to me even if all the cavemen in some tribe had sex with men on workdays and with women on holidays.

Yes, walking sticks, heterosexuals, homosexuals, and honest men *do* exist in nature—nature as understood in a particular context by a conceptual consciousness in fulfillment of a particular cognitive purpose.

Herek seems to understand that valid concepts start with reality when he writes that "our notions of heterosexuals and homosexuals" are "created," "starting from the raw material of humans' inherent ambisexuality and inevitable development of erotic and affectional preferences." But he does not seem to understand that valid concepts retain their connection to reality. He instead seems to believe that the very process of conceptualization severs the objective connection to reality and results in subjectivity, because—following Kant and Hegel—he conceives conceptualization as a non-rational process of "creation" or "construction" by a collective of minds.

But the presence of a rational mind in the conceptual process does not destroy objectivity. As I write elsewhere (Pisaturo 2020, 70),

> As epistemological or cognitive terms, "objective" does not refer to an object apart from a subject, and "subjective" does not refer to a subject apart from an object. Instead, both "objective" and "subjective" are relational and volitional terms; each term refers to a different kind of relation that an individual can choose to have between object and subject.
>
> To be objective is to recognize that the causal interaction between existence and consciousness, for the purpose of cognition, depends on the nature of both.

(See Ayn Rand [1966–1967] 1990 for the Objectivist theory of concepts, establishing the basis of objectivity. See also Pisaturo 2020 for my theory of an objective epistemology, drawing heavily from Ayn Rand's theory of concepts.)

Note also that Herek cites the most barbaric practices of primitive tribes to call into question the concepts of our advanced, civilized society. If some concepts of contemporary society need to be challenged—concepts such as "social construction" and "psychologist," for instance—the rational way to do so is by referring to reality, not by referencing barbaric, primitive, irrational societies. I do not need to mention—nor does it further my argument to mention—that some cave man did not have the notion of "social construction" in order for me to show that the notion is absurd. (Comically, these same tribal examples show up in article after article advocating the "social construction" of sexual orientation.)

Now we come to an ethical point. What does this argument for social construction let Herek and his ilk get away with? It lets them change the subject, that is, evade the issue. Instead of addressing the question of whether all sexual orientations are equally life-affirming, and instead of identifying the intellectual premises underlying each sexual orientation, the social constructionists challenge the very *idea* of "sexual orientation." And who came up with the idea of sexual orientation? According to the social constructionists, heterosexuals did, because male heterosexuals control our society and use the notions of sexual orientation and masculinity to maintain control. And so instead of trying to understand homosexuality, Herek can spend the remainder of his article—and career, judging by the rest of his work—writing about what is allegedly wrong about heterosexuals and masculinity.

Herek writes ([1986] 1993, 320–321),

> Heterosexual masculinity embodies personal characteristics such as success and status, toughness and independence, aggressiveness and dominance.
>
> ...
>
> In recent years writers have pointed out the maladaptive aspects of heterosexual masculinity in terms of physical health, personal health, and psychological happiness.

(In the next chapter, I will discuss the connection between the philosophy of the LGBT movement and such criticisms of masculinity.)

And that is the pattern of most academic writing about sexual orientation. Homosexuals are considered healthy victims; male heterosexuals are considered oppressors; and writers psychologize about the alleged neuroses of the oppressors, most of whom the psychologizers have never met, but about whom they collect data from polls and multiple-choice questionnaires. (See, for example, Herek [1986] 1993, 317–318).

In the same article, Herek ([1986] 1993, 318) writes,

> Another set of empirical findings concerns the role of defensiveness in homophobia [an alleged neurotic fear that heterosexuals have of homosexuals, allegedly often due to the heterosexuals fearing that they themselves have homosexual feelings]. In psychodynamic terms, defensiveness involves an unconscious distortion of reality as a strategy for avoiding recognition of some unacceptable part of self. One mode of defense is externalization of unacceptable characteristics through projection and other strategies.

If I were to use Herek's method of psychologizing about individuals I have never met, I could state that he—a homosexual—is projecting his unacceptable homosexuality onto heterosexuals; but I have no evidence that his evasion of the rational study of sexual orientation is unconscious.

The ethical point in short is that the notion of "social construction" is simply an evasion to avoid the judging of homosexuality.

It gets worse, or at least it gets more explicit. In the same article, Herek ([1986] 1993, 320) writes,

> The social constructionist position holds that what most people call reality is a consensus worldview that

develops through social interaction (see Berger and Luckmann 1966; Foucault 1978; Gergen 1985, Plummer 1981). [Underlined emphasis added.]

Thus, Herek here reveals explicitly what I showed was implicit in his appeal to primitive tribes: Herek is arguing that not merely is it sexual orientation that is socially constructed, and not merely is it all of sexuality that is socially constructed, but all of reality is socially constructed.

Following the suggestion of Herek to see his references, I saw the first three references he cites just above.

In Foucault's 1978 book, *The History of Sexuality, Volume I: An Introduction*, cited favorably by Herek, I found this ripple of semi-lucidity amidst muddy waters (p. 105–106):

> Sexuality must not be thought of as a kind of natural given which power tries to hold in check, or as an obscure domain which knowledge tries gradually to uncover. It is the name that can be given to a historical construct: not a furtive reality that is difficult to grasp, but a great surface network in which the stimulation of bodies, the intensification of pleasures, the incitement to discourse, the formation of special knowledges, the strengthening of controls and resistances, are linked to one another, in accordance with a few major strategies of knowledge and power.

Thus, according to Foucault, as according to Herek, it is not merely sexual orientation that is a social construct; rather, *sexuality*—in all the irrational banality that Foucault attributes to it—is a social construct.

And here is how Foucault's book ends (1978, 159):

> Christianity once employed to make us detest the body; but let us ponder all the ruses that were employed for

centuries to make us love sex, to make the knowledge
of it desirable and everything said about it precious. Let
us consider the stratagems by which we were induced
to apply all our skills to discovering its secrets, by
which we were attached to the obligation to draw out
its truth, and made guilty for having failed to recognize
it for so long. These devices are what ought to make us
wonder today. Moreover, we need to consider the possibility that one day, perhaps, in a different economy of
bodies and pleasures, people will no longer quite understand how the ruses of sexuality, and the power that
sustains its organization, were able to subject us to that
austere monarchy of sex, so that we became dedicated
to the endless task of forcing its secret, of exacting the
truest of confessions from a shadow.

The irony of this deployment is in having us believe
that our "liberation" is in the balance.

Thus, the conclusion that sexual orientation is unimportant is
based on a conclusion that *sexuality* is unimportant, that sexuality is
a mere "shadow." Thus we arrive at a sexual nihilism more complete
than the sexual nihilism of the biological determinists.

I also "saw" Berger and Luckmann's 1966 book, *The Social Construction of Reality*, cited favorably by Herek, and found these passages:

Berger and Luckmann 1966, 13:

The basic contentions of the argument of this book are
implicit in its title and sub-title, namely, that reality is
socially constructed and that the sociology of
knowledge must analyse the process in which this occurs.

Berger and Luckmann 1966, 15:

It is from Marx that the sociology of knowledge derived its root proposition—that man's consciousness is determined by his social being.

Berger and Luckmann 1966, 69:

As soon as one observes phenomena that are specifically human, one enters the realm of the social. Man's specific humanity and his sociality are inextricably intertwined. Homo sapiens is always, and in the same measure, homo socius. [Recall the quotation of Frumkin: "he becomes a human, social being."]

Berger and Luckmann 1966, 209:

The insight into the dialectic between social reality and individual existence in history is by no means new. It was, of course, most powerfully introduced into modern social thought by Marx. What is needed, however, is to bring to bear a dialectical perspective upon the theoretical orientation of the social sciences.

Then I "saw" Gergen's 1985 article, cited favorably by Herek, entitled "The Social Constructionist Movement in Modern Psychology," and found this (p. 271–272):

What is confronted, then, is the traditional, Western conception of objective, individualistic, ahistoric [that is, fundamental enough to be independent of time and place] knowledge—a conception that has insinuated itself into virtually all aspects of modern institutional life. As this view is increasingly challenged one must entertain the possibility of molding an alternative scientific metatheory based on constructionist assumptions. ...

Elsewhere, the contours of this emerging metatheory have been referred to as sociorationalist (Gergen, 1982;

Gergen & Morawski, 1980). In this view the locus of
scientific rationality lies not within the minds of independent persons but within the social aggregate. That
which is rational is the result of negotiated intelligibil-
ity.

This passage is written by an extremely influential *psychologist*
who does not know that the only kind of entity capable of rational
thought is an individual human being.

Thus, Herek's argument against sexual orientation is an argument against all of reason and reality, from which the argument
against sexual orientation is a trivial deduction.

Can it get worse? I don't know, but here is more from the same
one article by Herek. He writes ([1986] 1993, 323),

Through intense political struggle, lesbians and gay
men have made considerable progress in shifting the
realm of discourse on sexual orientation from medicine
to civil liberties (e.g. see Altman 1982; D'Emilio 1983).

I have already quoted D'Emilio at length. Here are some passages
from Altman's 1982 book, *The Homosexualization of America: The
Americanization of The Homosexual*, cited favorably by Herek:
Altman 1982, 41:

Any discussion of sexuality must balance the contribu-
tion to our behavior and emotions of inborn desire and
of social constructs.

This author too is writing about all of sexuality, not merely sexual
orientation.
Altman 1982, 41:

Biology and culture are not alternatives, but rather dual
factors that interact with each other to produce particular expressions of sexuality. Such sexual expressions
can take many and varied forms (including abstinence),

but ultimately they involve a universal need for body contact, erotic stimulation, and orgasmic release.

There is no mention of love or values.
Altman 1982, 184:

> Once sex is desacrilized and separated from its procreative function, it becomes evident that there is no reason to regard it as a form of behavior set apart from others. If it is regarded as legitimate to have a meaningful discussion with someone one meets on a voyage and will never see again, why cannot it be equally meaningful to have a f--- with someone in similar circumstances? [Literal obscenity removed.]

Altman 1982, 185, favorably quoting Rita Mae Brown:

> I want the option of random sex with no emotional commitment when I need sheer physical relief: erotic freedom.

Altman 1982, 200:

> One might also argue that since no one advocates preventing all interaction between children and adults, it is making too much of sex to argue that this relationship alone should be prohibited.

Altman 1982, 201:

> If sexuality were free from the sorts of pressures that exist in our society—it would be utopian to argue for *no* social pressures that exist in our society—I suspect child/adult sex would be fairly common, though not perhaps as common as sex among children themselves.

In response to these sordid—and evil—calls for promiscuity and mindlessness to the point of sexual nihilism and extreme abuse of children, I offer these words of Cyrano de Bergerac (Rostand [1898] [1923] 1980):

P. 77

> Watching you other people making friends
> Everywhere—as a dog makes friends! I mark
> The manner of these canine courtesies
> And think: "My friends are of a cleaner breed;
> Here comes—thank God!—another enemy!"

P. 110:

> ... It is my voice, mine, my own,
> That makes you tremble, as a blossom
> Among the leaves—You tremble, and I can feel,
> All the way down along these jasmine branches,
> Whether you will or no, the passion of you
> Trembling...
> *(He kisses wildly the end of a drooping spray of jasmine.)*

> Roxane
> Yes, I do tremble...and I weep...
> And I love you...and I am yours...and you
> Have made me thus!

Aside from Ayn Rand, Peikoff, and Rostand, all of the quotations in this section are from leading mainstream academic researchers in psychology and/or sexuality.

In short, contemporary academia and psychology believe that the etiology of sexual orientation has no basis in rational ideas because they believe that *sexuality* has no basis in rational ideas.

Whatever one thinks of the healthfulness of homosexuality, the psychological professions certainly are very sick indeed.

But etiology is only one aspect of the study of sexual orientation. Let us see how philosophical ideas affect other aspects of research regarding sexual orientation.

5. LGBT IDEOLOGY: EVASION PROPPED UP BY NEW-LEFT SUBJECTIVISM

In the previous chapter, I identified that, within the psychological professions, the mainstream defense of sexual orientations other than heterosexuality reduces to sexual nihilism.

In the first half of this chapter, I identify several "elephants in the room": basic issues—including glaring hypocrisies—that the psychological professions and LGBT activists systematically evade. In the second half, I identify the ideology that encourages such evasions and hypocrisies. This ideology, as we shall see, reduces to nihilism toward all Western values.

The Evasions

Consider this passage:

> There is good reason to believe that for many women, feelings of sexual attraction are less fixed and more flexible than originally thought. ... Some women could be having relationships with members of both sexes at the same time. In fact, only one third of the women who initially identified as lesbians at the start of the re- search project reported exclusive sexual attractions and behavior toward women over the course of the study.
> ...
> There is evidence that male sexual attractions and be- haviors can also be fluid.

This passage is from a recent article—by professor, psychothera- pist, and homosexual Michael C. LaSala—in *Psychology Today* entitled "Sexual Orientation: Is It Unchangeable?" (LaSala 2011). (Let us leave aside, until later, the implicit tolerance of promiscuity in this passage.) The article expresses the now-prevalent view, among professionals in psychology, that sexual orientation is not fixed at birth or at a young age, but rather can change back and forth even in adulthood.

Nevertheless, many psychological professionals are against the idea of patients questioning their current sexual orientation. In other words, it is acceptable for sexual orientation to change on its own, as if by magic, but it is not acceptable for an individual to try to understand why his current sexual orientation might change or perhaps should change. Davison (1991, 139) offers a popular defense of this apparent hypocrisy:

> The very naturalness of what therapists agree to do
> with particular kinds of cases tends to blind them to
> their prejudices and biases. ... [B]iases play a control-
> ling role in what is done [by the therapist]. This seems
> to be particularly the case in the approach to those peo-
> ple who have homosexual behavior or feelings.

In other words, according to Davison, a therapist should not help patients question their homosexuality—even though sexual orientation is highly changeable—because the therapist cannot trust his own biases against homosexuality. Davison (1991, 148) concludes,

> I have argued that change-of-orientation therapy pro-
> grams are ethically improper and should be eliminated.
> Their availability only confirms professional and socie-
> tal biases against homosexuality, despite seemingly pro-
> gressive rhetoric about its normality.

This argument closes the door on the possibility of a therapist questioning the homosexuality of any particular patient, regardless of the reason that the particular patient is homosexual. If a therapist does question a particular patient's homosexuality, the therapist's professional peers accuse him of being unethical, on the grounds that any therapist is incapable of objectivity. But on such a premise, every therapist is unethical simply by practicing therapy.

Hypocritically, though many psychological professionals who "affirm" homosexuality are themselves homosexual, no one in the profession questions *their* objectivity.

Now consider these passages from a mainstream scholarly work:

> Briefly summarized, the homosexual is definitely emotionally disturbed, suffering from fear of the other sex, puritanical distortions about sexuality, self-abnegation, feelings of inadequacy, self-destructive drives, and compulsive desires.
>
> ...
>
> It is quite natural that homosexuals, searching for an alleviation of the great stigma that attaches to their lives, would wish to convince themselves and the public that therapy is impossible, or almost so.
>
> ...
>
> The aim of therapy is to relieve the hostility toward and fear of relationships, sexual and other, with the other sex, rather than to seek to suppress the homosexual interests. The reasons for this are twofold: (1) to aid the homosexual to get at the root of the problem, and not to attack what is merely a symptom—his problem is not so much that he is attracted to males, but that he is in flight from females; and (2) to assure the homosexual that whatever pleasures and gratifications he is deriving from his present mode of life will not be removed, but if anything will be increased ... .

To anyone who has studied the subject of sexual orientation, it should be obvious that this passage is from an old work, because the

ideas expressed are now professionally taboo. The passages are by
Donald Webster Cory (1961, 491–492) in the entry entitled "Homosexuality" in *The Encyclopedia of Sexual Behavior*. Cory wrote extensively on his observations of homosexuals, and numerous psychological professionals made similar generalizations based on their
own in-person, in-depth psychoanalyses and similar studies of hundreds or even thousands of homosexuals. Consider, for example, this
passage from Bieber (1987, 422):

> The psychoanalyses of adult homosexuals reveals that
> they perceive other men in two ways: as aggressors who
> are feared and identified with the father, successful
> brothers, and combative peers; and as nonaggressors
> and as homosexuals like themselves who are not feared.
> This division enables them to come into a relationship
> with men, men who need not be defended against. Re-
> lationships with women in adult life are more trustful
> and positive, as long as the possibility of sex and ro-
> mance is excluded. The fear is that a heterosexual at-
> tempt will elicit a dangerous, even lethal attack by com-
> bative men.

Regarding a 1962 study by Bieber and numerous other researchers (see Bieber et al. 1988), Bieber (1987, 424) writes,

> Of the 106 homosexuals who started psychoanalytic
> therapy, 29 were exclusively heterosexual at the time
> the volume was published. This represented 27% of the
> total sample. Fourteen of these 29 had been exclusively
> homosexual when they began treatment: 15 were bisex-
> ual. In 1965, in a follow-up study of the 29, I was able to
> reclaim the data on 15 of the 29. Of these 15 men,
> twelve had remained exclusively heterosexual; the other
> three were predominantly heterosexual, but had occa-
> sional episodes of homosexuality when under severe

stress. Of the twelve who had remained consistently heterosexual, seven had been among the 14 who had been exclusively homosexual when they started treatment. Thus, seven men who started treatment as exclusively homosexual had been exclusively heterosexual for at least six or seven years.

That is, Bieber—although a Freudian and perhaps placing insufficient emphasis on volition—identified and helped some of his patients correct harmful conclusions that they had reached and that, according to Bieber, had led to their homosexuality.

As reported in Chapter 3, homosexual activists stalked, harassed, and sought to discredit Bieber (a "nonaggressor," as Bieber might categorize himself), and such activists have sought ever since to forbid any kind of work that questions the merit of homosexuality.

The main objections to such studies as Beiber's have always been that they were on unrepresentative samples of the general population. (See, for example, Gonsiorek 1991, 120–127.) Such objections have also been accompanied by opposing citations of mere multiple-choice questionnaires and Rorschach tests, without actual in-person psychological analyses. (Recall my references, in Chapter 3, to Gonsiorek 1991.) Another objection has been that psychoanalysts were biased against homosexuality. (See, for example, Gonsiorek 1991, 117–120). Regarding Bieber's 1962 study in particular, Gonsiorek (1991, 127) writes,

> There are two many sources of potential research bias in this research. [Underlined emphasis added.]

In response to the objection that his original sample was of a white, middle- and upper-class population, Bieber (1988, 418) writes,

> In the many years since our volume was published, I have interviewed more that 1,000 male homosexuals in

psychoanalytically focused psychiatric interviews. I
have also interviewed about 75 pairs of parents of patients. In all regards, the data were in accord with the
findings reported in our volume [of 1962]. Most subjects in this large sample were interviewed at a city hospital, came from a lower socio-economic strata, and belonged to one of three ethnic groups: Black, Puerto Ri-
can, or white, distributed about evenly.

Even granting the objection of unrepresentative samples, and
granting the (unsubstantiated) objection that not all homosexuals
can be accurately described by the passages by Cory and/or Bieber
above, and granting that some researchers might "potentially" have
been biased, it is implausible that no homosexuals or even that only
a few homosexuals fit Cory's and/or Bieber's descriptions. Indeed,
the work of Bieber in particular provides strong evidence for my own
theory that sexual orientation is caused by an individual's conclusions, which are drawn volitionally.

In contrast to Gonsiorek's (1991, 135) standard of "adjustment"
(see Chapter 3), Bieber (1988, 426) writes,

Behavior is psychologically abnormal when it is based
on irrational or unrealistic fears. In the case of homosexuality, as I have emphasized, the fears are of hostile
responses by other men, should heterosexual, romantic
wishes be fulfilled.

Any reasonable assessment of the testimony of numerous psychiatrists having had clinical experience with numerous homosexuals
leads to the incontestable conclusion that many homosexuals fit
Cory's and/or Bieber's descriptions above. Yet, in all the mainstream
academic literature from the past four decades, I did not find one
article or book that discussed a problem connected to homosexuality
that was not allegedly caused by society. In particular, I did not find
one mention of any homosexual having a fear of women or men. (If

anyone knows of such references, please let me know.) The only explanation for such an omission is evasion on a grand scale encompassing entire professions.

LGBT advocates often claim—see for example, Davison 1991, 137—that there is a double standard against homosexuals: that homosexuals are always doubted and scrutinized, whereas heterosexuals are always accepted as normal. In the academic literature, the precise opposite double standard exists. Though it is taboo to write about the possibility of a homosexual man being afraid of women, or of men who would fight them over women as was theorized by Bieber, there is article after article, book after book, career after career of "psychologizing"—on the basis of speculation without actual, in-depth examination of individuals—about heterosexual men having a neurotic fear of other men, especially homosexual men. (See Ayn Rand's essay, 'The "Psychology of Psychologizing," for an explanation of the term "psychologizing.") We all know the word for this alleged fear of homosexuals: "homophobia."

In my preparation for this book in 2015, a Google search of the words "gynophobia" and "gynephobia," denoting an irrational fear of women, returned about 84,000 and 31,000 results, respectively. In contrast, "homophobia" returned more than 9,500,000 results.

The term "homophobia" was coined by George Weinberg, a psychotherapist, in his book *Society and the Homosexual* (1972). Weinberg describes "homophobia" as a "disease" (1972, unnumbered third page of preface) and "the dread of being in close quarters with homosexuals" (1972, 4); Weinberg (2012) also describes homophobia as "the irrational fear of gay people."

Weinberg (1972, 1) also writes,

> The person who belittles homosexuals with evident enjoyment is at the very least telling me that he wants to establish his own sense of importance through contrast with other people—a tenuous business.

Weinberg then tells a sordid tale of heterosexual men deliberately taking their wives or girlfriends to see homosexual stage shows in order to show off their own heterosexuality in contrast. Weinberg (1972, 2) then continues,

> This is the identity that the patient who slurs homosexuality assumes in my mind while he is talking. He is bracing himself and trying to bolster his relationship by presenting it against a contrast.

Yet hypocritically, Weinberg (2012) wrote the following in an article in the *Huffington Post*:

> For gay people everywhere, the term "homophobia" became a reminder of their personal worth. Understanding that homophobia is at work in their tormentors gave gay people a new sense of dignity and humanity.

Not surprisingly, Weinberg (2012) continues to oppose alleged injustice by advocating injustice:

> [T]he Associated Press, in the latest update of its stylebook for reporters, banned the use of the word "homophobia" on the grounds that it suggests emotional disturbance in people when we allegedly have no proof of such disturbance.
>
> ...
>
> By the AP's logic -- that we cannot attribute motive where we haven't proved it -- we would have to get rid of terms like "hate crime," but no one suggests that. [I do more than "suggest" that. "Hate crimes" are Orwellian "crimes" of thoughts and feelings.]
>
> It is a curious decision to shun the word "homophobia" when there is no other word that does the same job. No other word suggests that the problem is in those who persecute gay people. As long as homophobia exists, as

long as gay people suffer from homophobic acts, the word will remain crucial to our humanity. Indeed, the next big step should be to add "homophobia" to the official list of mental disorders -- not to cleanse the language of it.

Here is an example of what Weinberg (1972, unnumbered first page of preface) evidently considers persecution of homosexuals:

> At present, it is not unconstitutional to deny housing to a person who is a known homosexual, or to refuse a job to such a person for this reason. ...
>
> Such discriminatory practices against homosexuals have deep psychological motives ...

Thus, for my *ideas*, the idea of individual rights along with my ideas regarding romantic love, Weinberg would psychologize about me—and about Thomas Jefferson, for that matter—and call me mentally diseased.

The LGBT movement's use of the term "homophobia" is a smoking gun revealing that the movement is not only irrational; it is dishonest. LGBT activists take their own (sexual) feelings as irreducible primaries that must be "affirmed" by everyone. Yet, hypocritically, they condemn heterosexuals for the *heterosexuals'* feelings. Calling people "homophobic" is psychologizing that these people are neurotic, while complaining that these people call others neurotic.

On the last page of his book, Weinberg (1972, 143) "warns" homosexuals against attempting to convert from homosexuality, concluding as follows:

> Your attempt to convert is an assault on your right to give and receive love, or sensual pleasure without love, in the manner you wish to. [Underlined emphasis added.]

The second underlined phrase reveals that Weinberg is a sexual subjectivist who endorses promiscuity. (Keep in mind that Weinberg was a long-time practicing *psychotherapist*.) But consider the first underlined phrase. Imagine the reaction by LGBT activists if a heterosexual man warned a second heterosexual man that the second man would be assaulting his own rights by exploring the possibility of being homosexual. Yet Weinberg issues the ominous threat above against any homosexual who would consider the possibility of being heterosexual.

Weinberg (1972, 41–68) and others argue that past methods to convert sexual orientation—methods based on absurd, Freudian assumptions—have a bad track record of success. Some also argue that it is no use trying to understand the cause of one's sexual orientation if the orientation cannot change anyway. Leaving aside the fact that many LGBT advocates also claim—hypocritically—that sexual orientation is fluid, there is great value in understanding one's sexual orientation even if it could not change, especially if one's orientation is healthy. As I wrote in Chapter 1 (and explained further in Chapter 2), "By understanding his sex-specific evaluation and what that evaluation implies for his relationship with his romantic partner, a man (or woman) can learn to express his identity more consistently, more thoroughly, and more joyfully." Identifying the premises underlying one's sex-specific sexual values enables one to integrate mind and body with respect to one's sexual responses.

An individual who does not want to understand the cause of his sexual orientation is assuming that there is nothing good to be discovered about his sexual orientation.

In short, here is the situation we have in the academic world and in the psychological professions regarding the issue of sexual orientation. Any professional who questions the healthfulness of homosexuality is condemned as unethical, in accordance with the argument by Davison. And any individual who questions his own homosexuality is threatened as someone who is assaulting his own rights, in accordance with the argument by Weinberg. Despite its cries of victimhood, the LGBT movement is a large-scale gang of intellectual bullies—devoid of any actual evidence or logical arguments for their conclusions—who have driven, through intimidation and threats, most non-believers into the closet. Moreover, as I described in Chapter 3, the LGBT movement agitates government to force individuals to have economic and social intercourse with non-heterosexuals.

Then there are some writers, such as Herek (1993), who use the word "heterosexism" along with "homophobia." These writers define "heterosexism" as a prejudice in favor of heterosexuality over other sexual orientations, and they liken heterosexism to racism. But let us examine this analogy to racism. As a heterosexual man excludes men from his pool of possible romantic partners, so a homosexual man excludes women. On what basis does a homosexual man exclude half the world's population from consideration as a sexual partner? On what basis does he claim that such an exclusion—such a discrimination—should go unexamined? If sex is an important criterion, should he not try to understand it? And if sex is an unimportant criterion, like race, then isn't he being irrational for applying it?

If LGBT activists want to use the "racist" analogy, then they have to claim that homosexuals are like black racists, that heterosexuals are like white racists, and that black racism is just as good as white racism.

Now consider this popular "ice cream" analogy, used here by LaSala (2011):

> [W]e should be as accepting of a person who has a relationship with a man and then a woman as we would of someone who usually eats vanilla ice cream and then decides to start eating pistachio. So what?

From the context of a heterosexual, a more apt analogy would be to compare eating ice cream to having someone shove ice cream up your bottom. If anyone objects to my apt modification of the usual analogy, consider what such an objection confesses about the objector's own assessment of homosexuality.

The aptness of my modification reveals that those who psychologize about and otherwise criticize heterosexuals who find homosexuality disgusting are—at best—callously dropping the rational context of those they criticize. More often, they are trying to evade rational scrutiny of homosexuality by verbally attacking heterosexuals.

LaSala (2011) continues,

> Sex between two consenting adults, like eating ice
> cream, should be about pleasure, personal preferences,
> <u>or</u> expressions of love and affection, not about <u>social
> rules and definitions</u>. [Underlined emphasis added.]

Note the word "or." According to LaSala, sexual relations *might* be about love and affection, but do not have to be. Sexual relations might just be about pleasure or personal preferences, and that is as it should be, according to LaSala. It is no wonder that a mind such as LaSala's likens sexual activity to a casual pleasure such as eating ice cream.

Recall Ayn Rand's terms of "intrinsicism" and "subjectivism" as false alternatives, with the right course being objectivity. (See Peikoff 1991, 142 along with Chapter 4 of the present book.) To LaSala, the alternative to his subjectivism is the intrinsicist straw man of "social rules and definitions." (LGBT activists make much use of this straw man, conveniently furnished to them by various religions and the notion that the primary purpose of sex is procreation.) That there could be objective principles regarding sexual orientation or anything else about sexual values does not occur to someone such as LaSala. Not surprisingly, LaSala in the same article favorably mentions studies (without citations) that purport to identify sexual orientation based on responses to erotic videos. Recall my discussion in

Chapter 4 regarding such studies by Bailey, cited by LeVay, that assume that sexual responses are mindless.

Keep in mind that LaSala is a professor and psychotherapist who advises parents on how to deal with the issue of homosexuality with their children!

LaSala thus provides one more example of a defense of homosexuality devolving into a defense of subjectivity—indeed, subjectivity regarding sexuality itself—such defense mainly entailing an attack on straw men.

One more expression of callous subjectivism is the view, held by many LGBT advocates, that an individual should try various sexual orientations in order to discover which orientation he prefers. Thompson (2012, 13) reports this example:

> At a government school in Wisconsin, students were required to take a "Heterosexual Questionnaire" that asked them questions such as: "If you have never slept with someone of your same gender, then how do you know you wouldn't prefer it?"

Those with such a callous attitude toward sexual activity seem to have no conception of the damage that can be done from a single mindless and/or demeaning sexual experience. Perhaps such individuals also think that rape is no worse than shoplifting.

Now consider this passage (Cory, 1961, 489):

> Whatever form the physical expression may take, the sexual act is more likely to be frustrating for homosexuals, even for those who reach a climax, than a heterosexual act is for heterosexuals. This is because of physical obstacles to a satisfactory relationship (<u>lack of biologically complementing fit</u>), and because ... [Underlined emphasis added.]

Again, it is not surprising that this passage is more than fifty years old. Few contemporary writers address the incontrovertible physical problem of "lack of biologically complementing fit." The most candid acknowledgement of this problem I could find was this passage from Altman (1971, 78):

> Anatomy has forced the homosexual to explore the realities of polymorphous eroticism beyond the experiences of most heterosexuals, for we are denied the apparently "natural" navel-to navel coupling of men/women. There is among most homosexuals, I suspect, an awareness of their body, a knowledge of human sensuality, that is one of their strengths ... .

If a man born blind develops acute skills of listening, he is to be commended. But what of a man with healthy eyes who is told not to try to understand why they won't open?

Another evasion is the presenting of the false alternative between illness and affirmation. (This false alternative was introduced in Chapter 3.) Observe that LGBT activists have gone from claiming that homosexuals are not necessarily mentally ill to demanding that no one question a given individual's homosexuality—not even the homosexual individual himself. Defenders of homosexuality often argue (for example, Gonsiorek 1991, 19–20) that they need identify only one "healthy" homosexual to win their argument that homosexuality is just as good as heterosexuality. This argument fails on two counts.

First, in my study of the literature, researchers have not reasonably established the health of even one individual homosexual regarding his sexual orientation. Recall that in the widely-cited, supposedly definitive article—Gonsiorek 1991—allegedly proving that homosexuality is not necessarily an illness, there is not one reported instance of an actual professional actually examining the *thinking* of a person being "tested." There are only check marks on multiple-choice questionnaires and forms, and a few interpretations of ink blots.

But the second count of failure of this argument is far more important. The fundamental issue is not whether homosexuality is an illness. A far more fundamental issue is whether all sexual orientations are equally beneficial to human life. Recall the statement by the American Psychiatric Association (1973, 2–3) pursuant to its decision to remove homosexuality from its *Diagnostic and Statistical Manual of Mental Disorders* (DSM), quoted in Chapter 3 and restated in part below:

> by no longer listing [homosexuality] as a psychiatric disorder we are not saying that it is "normal" or as valuable as heterosexuality.
>
> ...
>
> No doubt, homosexual activist groups will claim that psychiatry has at last recognized that homosexuality is as "normal" as heterosexuality. They will be wrong.

The LGBT activists are not merely wrong. They are evading, and they have been evading since before this decision in 1973. It is an evasion to "affirm" one's sexual behavior merely on the grounds that one is not necessarily sick, as if to say, "I am not necessarily sick; therefore, anything I do is okay." "Sick"—whether necessarily or possibly—vs. "not sick" is not the right axis of measurement.

Now we come to an important philosophical evasion regarding the theory, now dominant in academic writing, that sexual orientation is "socially constructed." I found only one (partial) acknowledgment by LGBT activists that the theory of "social constructionism" is self-refuting. The acknowledgment occurs in an exchange between Richard Schneider, founder of *The Harvard Gay & Lesbian Review*, and David M. Halperin, a leading LGBT theorist and author of *One Hundred Years of Homosexuality* (1990). From that book (Halperin

1990, 53), here is a passage from a chapter entitled "'Homosexuality':
a Cultural Construct; An Exchange with Richard Schneider":

> *Schneider.* But isn't there a contradiction here? If ho-
> mosexuality is a cultural construct, and if such con-
> structs operate at the level of individual subjectivities to
> determine personal identity, how can any of us—in-
> deed, how can you—accept in any genuine sense the
> position that you are arguing for, a position that would
> seem to place whoever occupies it outside the cultural
> and sexual systems into which we were all born?
>
> *Halperin.* That's a very canny question, but I'm not
> ashamed of the awkward spot it puts me in. I would be
> very untrue to the position I've been arguing for if I
> didn't acknowledge squarely and forthrightly the cogni-
> tive dissonance it involves. I don't think there's any way
> that I, or anyone else who grew up in bourgeois Amer-
> ica when I did, could ever believe in what I've been say-
> ing with the same degree of conviction with which I be-
> lieve, despite everything I've said, in the categories of
> heterosexuality and homosexuality. ... So I freely admit
> that, in a sense, I don't, and couldn't possibly, *believe* in
> what I've been saying ...

Nevertheless, awareness of his contradiction does not stop
Halperin from writing more books on the subject. As we shall see,
LGBT theorists explicitly embrace the philosophical tradition of Hegel, Marx, and the Frankfurt School, which includes Marcuse. This
tradition, in turn, explicitly embraces contradictions through a He-
gelian process of "synthesis" of contradictions.

In summary, the psychological professions and academia systematically evade the following basic questions, hypocrisies, and contradictions regarding sexual orientation:

- Why do homosexuals discriminate against members of the opposite sex in their sexual responses? Why are many homosexuals actually afraid of and/or antagonistic toward the opposite sex and/or heterosexuals of the same sex?
- If sexual orientation is fluid, why do psychological professions condemn professionals and homosexuals for exploring the possibility of change?
- If psychological professionals cannot escape their own biases (an absurd premise dominant in the profession), why should homosexual professionals "affirm" homosexuality?
- If the sexual feelings of homosexuals must be "affirmed" by everyone, why shouldn't the feelings of heterosexuals—including their feelings of disgust for homosexuals—be "affirmed" by everyone?
- What problems for homosexuals arise from the "lack of biologically complementing fit"?
- Illness vs. "affirmation" is a false alternative.
- All the mainstream LGBT theories of etiology—biological determinism, social determinism, and social constructionism—are self-refuting.

LGBT Ideology

Instead of addressing these questions, hypocrisies, and contradictions, the LGBT movement adopts these two policies:

- Counter-attacks against their alleged oppressors (male heterosexuals).
- Militant subjectivism regarding all aspects of sexuality—indeed, regarding all aspects of civilization.

These two policies are hallmarks of the contemporary cultural and political Left. Not surprisingly, key figures in the LGBT movement explicitly extol a particular philosopher who advocated both of these policies: Herbert Marcuse, a key figure of the Frankfurt School.

The first policy—counter-attack against heterosexual men—can be described more generally as follows: Be unethical to others while claiming that others are unethical to you. In his article, "Herbert Marcuse, Philosopher of the New Left," Walsh (1970, 9[12]: 10) writes that according to Marcuse,

> Objectivity or neutrality is spurious because the game is rigged: "When a magazine prints side by side a negative and positive report on the FBI, it fulfills honestly the requirements of objectivity: however, the chances are that the positive wins because the image of the institution is deeply engraved in the minds of the people." [Marcuse, 1969, 98.]

> To reverse the trends, Marcuse declares, people should "get information slanted in the opposite direction." [Marcuse 1969, 99.]

This policy to "get information slanted in the opposite direction" explains why LGBT activists whitewash homosexuals while smearing heterosexuals as "homophobic."

Walsh (1970, 9[12]: 10) also writes,

> Marcuse demands that objectivity be forbidden to the communications media, that certain doctrines be prohibited and that certain groups be deprived of the rights of free speech and free assembly. The re-education of the majority, "may require apparently undemocratic means. This would include the withdrawal of toleration of speech and assembly from groups and movements which promote aggressive policies, armament, chauvinism, discrimination on the grounds of race and religion, or which oppose the extension of public services, social security, medical care, etc." [Marcuse 1969, 100.]

> According to dialectical logic, this intolerance would be a form of tolerance, liberating tolerance: "Liberating

tolerance, then, would mean intolerance of movements from the Right, and toleration of movements from the Left. ... it would extend to the stage of action as well as of discussion and propaganda, of deed as well as of word." [Marcuse 1969, 109.] Such liberating tolerance must include censorship, which would counteract the "false consciousness" by "stopping the words and images which feed this consciousness." [Marcuse, 169, 111.] "Moreover, the restoration of freedom of thought may necessitate new and rigid restrictions on teachings and practices in the educational institutions which, by their very methods and concepts, serve to enclose the mind within the established universe of discourse and behavior ..." [Marcuse 1969, 100–101.]

Walsh (1970 9: 9–10) gives an example of the teachings of Marcuse put into practice:

An activist graduate student at the University of Buffalo, interviewed in *The New York Times* of May 5, 1968, stated: "Do you know why the demonstrations and protest movements succeeded? Because we didn't play by the rules of the game. Our movement wasn't organized democratically. We kicked the Dow people off the campus though they had every right to be there. It was our unrepressed intolerance and thorough anti-permissiveness that brought our actions success. But who gave us the intellectual courage to be intolerant and unpermissive? I think Herbert Marcuse more than anyone. He is the New Left's professor."

This policy of censorship explains why LGBT activists complain of a "stigma" against homosexuality while intimidating, threatening, and even coercing heterosexuals to "affirm" all sexual orientations.

Now let us revisit the second policy of the LGBT movement: militant subjectivism regarding all aspects of sexuality.

The idea of "social constructionism," supported by the psychological leaders of the LGBT movement, explicitly starts with Kant's notion that unconscious structures of individual minds subjectively construct reality (this "reality" being Kant's notion of a "phenomenal world"); but the social constructionists slightly alter this Kantian idea by claiming instead (like Hegel) that this process of "construction" is performed not by individual minds but by society as a whole. (See Gergen 1985, 269–270.)

The psychological leaders (such as Herek and Peplau) rely heavily on writers in philosophy, sociology, and related fields (writers such as Foucault, Altman, Wolf, and Connell) who in turn rely on the Kantian tradition as it continued through Hegel, Marx, Freud, and Marcuse. The usual pattern is that writers in psychology favorably cite intermediate sources such as Foucault, Altman, and Wolf, and the intermediate sources favorably cite more primary sources such as Hegel, Marx, and Marcuse. Everyone favorably cites Freud (sometimes with modifications).

For example, Herek ([1986] 1993, 320) favorably cites the leading "social constructionist" (and sexual nihilist) philosopher Foucault (see Chapter 4 for details); Foucault in turn (in another work: [2008] 2010, 21) writes,

> It seems to me that the philosophical choice confronting us today is the following. We have to opt either for a critical philosophy which appears as an analytical philosophy of truth in general, or for a critical thought which takes the form of an ontology of ourselves, of present reality. It is this latter form of philosophy which from Hegel to the Frankfurt School, passing through Nietzsche, Max Weber and so on, which has founded a form of reflection to which, of course, I link myself insofar as I can.

(As of the writing of the second edition of the present book, the subjectivism of social constructionism has reached pandemic proportions in Western culture, in the form of postmodernism—see Hicks 2011 for a critical account—and "critical studies" including "critical race theory"—see Pluckrose and Lindsay 2020 for a critical account. The LGBT movement is an ongoing part of this pandemic.)

For clarity and concision, I will state the general LGBT theory in my own words before turning to lengthier passages by some of the theory's exponents.

The general LGBT theory is as follows. Infants are "polymorphously perverse," to use Freud's term. That is, an infant will be sexually excited by anyone and anything anywhere. Freud considered this infantile state an early stage of development. Marcuse and many LGBT activists, in contrast, consider this state the ideal end state for adults. According to Marcuse, people leave this ideal state only because they become repressed, limiting the kinds of sexual responses available to them. The repressed energy of such people becomes channeled into economic production. (I'm not kidding; this is the theory, and the psychological professions buy into it.) That is, productive work is the repressed alternative to blissful, indiscriminate sex. Capitalism, of course the system of greatest economic production, is hence also the system of greatest sexual repression. Heterosexual males, who dominate and oppress other groups under capitalism, are the most sexually repressed and therefore the most driven to production and to dominance over everyone else. The sexual repression and economic productiveness perpetrated by heterosexual males is codified in the socially constructed idea of masculinity. The oppression of women, by these men, is codified in the socially constructed idea of femininity, which entails submissive weakness and the oppressive task of raising children. According to the LGBT movement, the feminist movement figured all this out. And now the LGBT movement has figured out that heterosexual males oppress homosexual men as well as heterosexual women, because homosexual men threaten the notion of masculinity. The solution to this whole problem is to eradicate capitalism, masculinity, femininity, and families, with everyone returning to the polymorphous perversity of an infant, and with the community of such adult infants collectively in charge of rearing actual infants.

In the LGBT literature, one thing I have not found is an explanation of how any economic production will continue once all the sexual repression goes away.

Of course, this theory is absurd. An infant will put anything in its mouth, touch anything, and climb out any window. Through reason, a child learns to become selective in his actions. Anyone who thinks that selectivity in sexuality is a form of repression holds a premise that reason and emotion are in inevitable conflict.

Regarding the notion that productive work drains a man's capacity for sexual fulfillment, the exact opposite is true. A child is born with the capacity, but not the ability, to achieve sexual fulfillment. The greater a rational man's success at production, the greater is his self-esteem; and the greater becomes his desire and ability to achieve romantic and sexual fulfillment.

There is one more philosophical element that goes hand in hand with the LGBT theory that I summarized above. Modern researchers in psychology tend to eschew conceptual understanding and value judgments in favor of counting instances of various kinds of "behavior." From such a methodology, it is easy to move from the premise that many people exhibit various kinds of sexual behavior to the conclusion that all such behavior is normal and healthful. Modern researchers claim that their method of counting instances of behaviors is mathematical and scientific, and that this method avoids researchers' bias. In truth, this method is as scientific as using a fancy ruler to measure weight. What needs to be studied by psychology is the mind, not mere physical behavior.

Now let us read all of these ideas, which I have summarized above, straight from academic writers who espouse them. Working backwards, let us start with an account of the method of counting instances of behavior. This method is described in the following passage from Chall (1961, 31–33):

> To gain information on or about human sexual behavior, behavioral scientists use the same methods used to gain information about political, economic, esthetic, or other human behavior: indirect techniques. The major techniques used are interviews, questionnaires, content analyses, and scales. All of these techniques in the last analysis ask questions and receive answers. The answers a scientist receives are what he terms "observations."
>
> …
>
> The empirical-quantitative method, in contrast to the grand theory of a Havelock Ellis, a Sigmund Freud, the Vaertings, or of William I Thomas, seems dull, plodding, and unimaginative. But this method has produced tremendous advances in studying sexual phenomena by two approaches: conceptual and methodological. Conceptually, it has created a language describing sexual behavior that is relatively free of "normative" encumbrances and connotations. It perceives sexual behavior as based less on human values traditionally defined and more on frequency and functionality. [Underlined emphasis added.]

The author, writing more than fifty years ago, later indicates that he is not fully satisfied with the method he describes; but contemporary LGBT researchers evidently—see Chapter 3 and later—embrace it fully.

Now let us read the LGBT ideas—"polymorphous perversity," the alleged repression inherent in production and capitalism, the alleged oppression by heterosexual males, etc.—from some of the LGBT theorists themselves.

Recall that Altman is one of the writers cited by the leading psychologist Herek. Altman, in his book *Homosexual Oppression and Liberation* (1971, 70), writes,

> In this discussion I am particularly indebted to Marcuse for his explorations of the concepts of repression and liberation.

Altman (1971, 77) continues,

> [I]t is undoubtedly true that sexual repression was highly functional for the rise of capitalism and later industrialization which, at least in the early stages, demanded considerable repression in the interests of economic development.

Altman (1971, 78–79) later writes as follows. (The brackets and bracketed text in the following quotation are in the original.)

> Marcuse has observed in *Eros and Civilization* that: "Against a society which employs sexuality as a means for a useful end, the perversions uphold sexuality as an end in itself; they thus place themselves outside the domination of the performance principle [Marcuse's term for the particular variety of repression necessary for the organization of capitalism] and challenges its very foundations." ... In the context of a society based on rigorous repression of polymorphous and bisexual urges, the homosexual thus comes to represent a challenge to conventional norms. ...

Altman (1971, 79) then becomes more candid than many other LGBT activists, as he writes,

Still, even in Marcusian variation of Freudian thought, exclusive homosexuality represents a repression that is as great as exclusive heterosexuality … . Homosexuals who like to point out that "everyone is queer"—"either latent or blatant"—as one girl put it—rarely concede that "everyone" is equally "straight," and that to repress the one is as damaging as to repress the other. …

The repression of polymorphous perversity in Western societies has two major components: the removal of the erotic from all areas of life other than the explicitly sexual, and the denial of our inherent bisexuality. The latter in particular is bound up with the development of very clear-cut concepts of "masculine" and "feminine" that dominate our consciousness—and help maintain male supremacy. It is awareness of the socially imposed masculine/feminine dichotomy that especially characterizes the analyses associated with women's liberation.

"Women's liberation" is today called "feminism." Later, Altman (1971, 89) writes,

Men in America are drawn together, yet the more they are drawn the more they need to repress their feelings, and thus the undercurrent of violence that exists between men and that is turned outwards in the assertion of masculine dominance, whether vis-à-vis foreigners (Vietnam?), women, or other inferiors. The argument that men fight each other because they are unable to love each other is a version of Marcuse's formulation that aggression results from a failure to give sexuality free reign. I find this argument persuasive, in part because of my observation of homosexuals.

Altman (1971, 102) also writes,

There are great advantages for <u>children in communal living</u>, representing as it does a compromise between the tyranny of overpossessive parents and the repression of the typical educational system. It is also probably the really only effective way to break down the sex-role stereotypes into which the family structure tends to force us. The idea that a child "belongs" to his parents is a logical extension of <u>the cult of property</u>, only exceeded in horror by the concept that a child "belongs" to the state. [Underlined emphasis added.]

Ultimately, as Marcuse insists, liberation implies a new biological person ... "... who rejects the performance principles ... "

Recall that Altman is the same person who wrote this passage in the book (1982, 201) cited favorably by Herek ([1986] 1993, 323):

If sexuality were free from the sorts of pressures that exist in our society—it would be utopian to argue for *no* social pressures that exist in our society—I suspect child/adult sex would be fairly common, though not perhaps as common as sex among children themselves.

Presumably, Altman would give "children in communal living" plenty of opportunity to have sex with their communal caretakers. A page later, Altman (1971, 103) writes,

[A]s individuals come to a greater acceptance of their erotic/sexual being they tend to reject the "performance principle" that underlies the dominant ethos of property, competition and aggression. ... Only a socialism highly flavored by anarchism would seem to me consistent with sexual liberation ...

All of these ideas by Altman are mainstream in the academic psychological literature on sexual orientation. All of the writers I am quoting have been cited favorably, in mainstream articles and books on psychology, as authoritative sources without a hint of there being any controversy involved in any of these ideas. I could write a book many times as long as the present one simply by including similar quotations from countless other mainstream articles I have read.

In the interest of brevity, I will take just one article, from the mainstream professional psychological literature, and show how this one article exemplifies, directly states, and/or cites all of the LGBT arguments I have identified in this section.

In 2012, Oxford University Press published its "authoritative" *Handbook of Psychology and Sexual Orientation*, intended for use by professionals. This passage is from the publisher's description of the book:

> The first authoritative summary of its kind in this area, *Handbook of Psychology and Sexual Orientation* is the primary resource for the many researchers, including a new generation of investigators, who are continuing to advance understanding in this field. Volume editors Charlotte J. Patterson and Anthony R. D'Augelli, along with other leading experts, contribute an extraordinary review of contemporary psychological research and theory on sexual orientation in their specific fields of work. The book is divided in four parts: <u>Concepts, Theories, and Perspectives</u>; Development over the Life Course; Domains of Experience; and Communities and Contextual Issues. [Underlined emphasis added.]

The first of the four parts seemed, by its description, the most "conceptual" and "theoretical," so I read that part's chapter (Parsons and Grov 2012) on male homosexuality. The chapter begins as follows:

> In this chapter we review <u>seminal research</u> and theory regarding gay men's identities, their desires, and their

sexual behavior. First we discuss the emergence of the gay identity and describe how meanings of the "gay community" have changed in response to fluid social/political climates, HIV, and technology. Next we discuss the role of desire in gay men's sexual partnerships and behaviors, focusing on masculinity, <u>penis size</u>, and <u>semen/ejaculation</u>. Third, we elaborate on the array of sexual behaviors in which gay men engage and describe the various types of relationships that are common within gay partnerships. [Underlined emphasis added.]

This passage illustrates the smallness of the thinking of researchers—in particular, their use of survey data in place of conceptualization—in this field. The first of the three sections is a socio-historical account of the development of a "gay community"; and the last two sections consist of survey data on issues such as how many homosexuals like large penises (very many), how many of them have sex outside of their committed relationships (very many), and how many of them "exchange semen." I guess I initially had an old-fashioned idea about the meaning of the authors' phrase, "seminal research."

The only section of this purportedly theoretical article that suggests any theoretical significance is the part of the second section that discusses masculinity. Parsons and Grov (2012, 21) write,

For gay men, traditional masculinity (as opposed to femininity) is often a desired trait. In general, gay men not only prefer men who describe themselves as masculine, but not one participant in a study of gay male personal ads looking for sexual partners listed masculinity as an *undesired* trait in a partner ... . In contrast, when undesired partner traits were listed, they were always feminine traits.

This data is merely unscientific survey data, but at least it is intriguing. Here is what Parsons and Grov (2012, 21) conclude from this data:

> It has been suggested that such gay men want to achieve "hegemonic masculinity" or a culturally normative ideal of male behavior in order to overcome negative stereotypes about effeminate gay men ... .
>
> So, from where does such as strong desire and preference for masculinity and the perceived sexual roles of those who are more masculine/feminine come? "Gay men are not free to invent new objects of desire... ["any more than heterosexual men are—their"] choice of object is structured by gender order" (Connell, 1992, p. 747). ... The ideals of <u>hegemonic masculinity</u> shape gay men as much as they shape heterosexual men. ...
>
> Social pressures compel gay men to value masculinity and devalue femininity. [Underlined emphasis added.]

Parsons and Grov are claiming that the ideas of "masculinity" and "femininity," which they assume have been harmful to heterosexuals, have been harmful to homosexuals too. To psychological professionals, evidently, it is taboo to suggest that masculinity can have objective value.

Parsons and Grov (2012, 21) use the term "hegemonic masculinity" four times. The term is well known in psychology and sociology. According to Wikipedia, the most cited source for this term is R. W. Connell's book, *Gender and Power* (1987), which Parsons and Grov also cite.

Here is the main thesis of Connell 1987. Women in society are oppressed not only by economic class as claimed by mainstream Marxism, but by "gender class" too. The genders of masculinity and femininity are social constructions. One particular such construction, "hegemonic masculinity," defines a compliant form of femininity, "emphasized femininity." These constructions enable (heterosexual) men to dominate women (and homosexual men) on a global scale. But the only true biological difference between men and women is the difference regarding the role in procreation. One solution to the oppression by hegemonic masculinity is to deconstruct and then politically abolish or reconstruct—on the principle of equality as opposed to freedom—all notions of masculinity and femininity in all aspects of human life, including work, social interactions, clothing, choice of sexual partners, and sexual behaviors. The other solution is for individuals to flit from masculinity to femininity as if at a series of costume balls. (That's my metaphor.)

And here are some quotations from the book.

Connell, 1987, 183:

> There is an ordering of versions of femininity and masculinity at the level of the whole society ... Their interrelation is centered on a single structural fact, the global dominance of men over women.

Connell, 1987, 287:

> If the abolition of gender is a worthwhile goal, then it must be the abolition of gender as a social structure that is at issue. As defined in chapter 6 gender is ultimately the linking of fields of social practice to the reproductive division, the creation of a relevance. Its abolition would be, logically, a matter of disconnecting those fields. This implies no denigration or denial of biological difference; equally, no celebration of it. Difference between sexes would be simply a complementarity of function in reproduction, not a cosmic division or a social fate. There would be no reason for this to structure emotional relationships, so the categories heterosexual and homosexual would become insignificant.

There would be no reason for it to structure character, so femininity and masculinity would depart.

Such a future is implied in the deconstructionist wing of gay liberation theory, and as an ultimate goal is more convincing than as an immediate strategy. Its great virtue is that it eliminates the basis for gender inequalities. The way biological difference and similarity have got incorporated into structures of social inequality creates our dilemma about 'nature', not nature itself. Inequality is the basis of the social constitution of interests, which generate the practices that institutionalize injustices, the politics that defend them, the ideologies that justify them. <u>The concept of liberation is not about freedom, in the sense of lack of constraint on personal behaviour, so much as about equality.</u> [Underlined emphasis added.]

To those of you on Facebook who posted a photo of an "equal" sign in support of "same-sex marriage," this is the ideology that you supported.

Connell 1987, 288:

The logical consequence of deconstruction is open-ended variety. Marcuse's discussion of 'polymorphous perversity' in *Eros and Civilization* is not a bad summary of this conception, though with rules dismantled nothing can be defined as normative and hence nothing as 'perverse'.

Connell 1987, 292:

As a matter of fact, the core institutions of the contemporary structure of gender power cannot be torn down without a class politics, because those institutions fuse gender and class domination. As a matter of practice,

Masculine Power, Feminine Beauty

equality is difficult to contain; the origins of modern
feminist radicalism in the New Left show that. The his-
toric association between socialism and feminism,
however tense and ragged it has been, expresses a basic
truth about the global structure of inequality and what
social forces might dismantle it.

In short, LGBT activists want to coerce the entire world into going along with their charade, their eradication of masculinity and
femininity, their evasion of the Law of Identity.

At the time of the writing of his 1987 book, R. W. Connell was a
man. Now Connell is a transsexual "woman," Raewyn Connell.

Getting back to the article by Parsons and Grov (2012) in Oxford
University Press's "authoritative" *Handbook of Psychology and Sexual Orientation*, recall that the article began with a historical account
of the emergence of a "gay community" (2012, 19):

Throughout history, homosexual behavior has been regarded in many ways, ranging from abhorrent to
revered (Wolf 2004). The idea of a gay community and
identifying oneself as "gay" is a concept that emerged,
as D'Emilio (1983) proposed, as a result of the Indus-
trial Revolution and the spread of capitalism throughout Europe and the United States. [Underlined emphasis added.]

This passage may seem innocuous, but let us examine the sources
that the authors cite: "Wolf 2004" and "D'Emilio 1983."

The article referenced as "Wolf 2004" is "The Roots of Gay Oppression", by Sherry Wolf, in the *International Socialist Review*. Here
is how Wolf 2004 begins:

Gay oppression hasn't always existed, and neither have
gays as a distinct sector of the population. The oppression of gays and lesbians—and all sexual minorities—is

one of modern capitalism's infinite contradictions. Capitalism creates the material conditions for men and women to lead autonomous sexual lives, yet it simultaneously seeks to impose heterosexual norms on society to secure the maintenance of an economic, ideological, and sexual order.

In the quotation above, Wolf (a Marxist) sets up a Marxist "dialectic"—a conflict of alleged contradictions in reality—that she claims are inherent in capitalism. To a Marxist such as Wolf, some aspects of capitalism were "progressive" over what preceded capitalism, but the contradictions of capitalism can be resolved—"synthesized"—only by further progress: socialism.

The article referenced as "D'Emilio 1983" is "Capitalism and Gay Identity", by Marxist historian John D'Emilio, who specializes in the history of homosexuality. Like Wolf, D'Emilio holds that a contradictory "dialectic" inherent in capitalism can be resolved only by socialism. This is from D'Emilio's ([1983] 1999, 48) preface to this article:

I wanted to be able to ground social construction theory, which posited that gay identity was historically specific rather than universal, in concrete social processes. Using Marxist analyses of capitalism, I argue that two aspects of capitalism – wage labor and commodity production – created the social conditions that made possible the emergence of a distinctive gay and lesbian identity.

And this is from the article by D'Emilio ([1983] 1999, 54) that Parsons and Grov cite:

[C]apitalism ... needs to push men and women into families, at least long enough to reproduce the next generation of workers. The elevation of the family to

ideological preeminence guarantees that a capitalist society will produce not just children, but heterosexism
and homophobia. In the most profound sense, capitalism is the problem.

In summary, all of the above works are cited as non-controversial
sources in one leading chapter (Parsons and Grov 2012) of Oxford
University Press's "authoritative" *Handbook of Psychology and Sexual Orientation*. This one chapter includes all of the philosophical
elements of LGBT theory that I identified at the beginning of this
section.

Sherry Wolf, who was cited by Parsons and Grov (2012), also
wrote a book entitled *Sexuality and Socialism*. Here is a passage from
that book (2009, 75):

Contrary to the dominant myth of socialism prevalent
in the academy, Marxists do not reduce the oppression
of sexual minorities—or anyone else—to the issue of
class. Rather, Marxists locate the source of racial, gender, sexual, and all other oppressions within the frame-
work of capitalist class relations. As the earlier discussion of the nuclear family showed, women's oppression
derives from the structure of the family, in which reproduction and maintenance (child care, housework,
cooking, etc.) of the current and future generations of
workers are foisted upon individual families rather
than being the responsibility of society. Capitalism depends on privatized reproduction to raise the next generation of workers at little expense to itself. Likewise,
the oppression of LGBT people stems from the implicit
challenge that sexual minorities pose to the nuclear
family and its gender norms.

What kind of human being thinks that parents' giving birth to
and caring for their child is something "foisted upon" the parents?

To those of you on Facebook who posted a photo of an "equal" sign, this is the ideology that you have allowed to be "foisted upon" you.

No discussion of the philosophy of the LGBT movement would be complete without mentioning the movement's big (ugly) sister: feminism. Observe that favorable references to feminism appear often in the quotations above, but that is just a start.

In the first edition of their highly regarded book, *Psychological Perspectives on Lesbian & Gay Male Experiences*, the editors Garnets and Kimmel (1983, 53) begin the second paragraph of their introduction to the topic, "The Meaning of Sexual Orientation" as follows:

> One particularly important influence in the process of reconceptualizing sexual orientation from an individual pathology to membership in a supportive community has been the feminist movement.

Many, many other mainstream articles and books I have read on psychology, in my research for the present book, praise the feminist movement; none of these writings offers a single word of criticism of feminism.

In his article "Gender Tribalism," Peter Schwartz (1998, 205–216) presents a thorough refutation and condemnation of feminism. To all the sources that Schwartz cites, let me add this one quotation of feminist philosopher Sally Haslanger (1993, 85), which captures the essence of the feminist movement:

> One of the common themes in feminist research over the past decade has been the claim that reason is "gendered": more specifically, that reason is "male" or "masculine." Although feminists have differed in their interpretations of this claim and the grounds they offer for it, the general conclusion has been that feminist theory should steer clear of investments in reason and rationality, at least as traditionally conceived. For example,

we should avoid an epistemology that privileges reason
or the standpoint of reason; we should avoid theories of
the self that take rationality to be a defining trait; and
we should avoid endorsing moral and political ideals
that glorify reason and the reasonable "person" (read:
man).

At the end of this article, Haslanger (a professor of philosophy at
the Massachusetts Institute of Technology) concludes that women
should reject reason, because accepting reason would be a form of
collaborating with the enemy: man.

This essay by Haslanger has been reprinted in Haslanger's book,
published by Oxford University Press, entitled *Resisting Reality: Social Construction and Social Critique* (2012).

The feminist movement is a caricature of a cartoon of an ideology. It is an evil cartoon. The essential evil of feminists is a refusal to
judge individual men or to be judged individually by them. Feminists
are willing to become subhuman, by rejecting reason, rather than
acknowledge any value created by man.

The LGBT movement is essentially an unoriginal caricature of
the feminist movement. Instead of depicting man as the oppressor of
women, the LGBT movement depicts heterosexual man as the oppressor of everyone else.

Since the publication of the first edition of the present book, the
LGBT movement has added more letters and a symbol to its initial-
ism. As of this writing, one of several popular initialisms is
LGBTQIA+. But as "people of color" (POC) simply means non-
whites, or anti-whites, LGBTetc simply means anti-H—that is, anti-
heterosexual.

In summary, the goal of LGBT activists is to eradicate masculinity
and femininity from society, and thereby eradicate all possibility of
being judged for their sexual identity. More broadly, the LGBT activists are bent on destroying all Western values, including reason,
productiveness, and capitalism.

As a final anecdote, I did find one ironical instance of a mainstream researcher in psychology attributing a certain sexual orientation to a set of ideas. Peplau (2001, 10) writes approvingly that

> ... active involvement in the 1970s feminist movement led some women to turn away from sexual relations with men and to establish relationships with women (e.g., Kitzinger, 1987). Pearlman (1987) explained that "many of the new, previously heterosexual, radical lesbians had based their choice as much on politics as on sexual interest in other women" (p. 318).

So here is an instance of a mainstream psychological researcher claiming that sexual orientation is not mindless. Well, perhaps not.

Now we are ready to address the relationship of sex-specific sexual evaluation to the concept of marriage.

6. MARRIAGE AS HETEROSEXUAL

Marriage is a legally sanctioned, publicly declared, exclusive and—by intention—permanent romantic relationship between a man and a woman, such relationship establishing each of the individuals as the other's next of kin, establishing rights and mutual responsibilities regarding joint property, and establishing rights and responsibilities regarding custody and care of the couple's children.

I do not think that procreation is the fundamental purpose of a romantic relationship or of marriage. Indeed, traditional marriage vows include much language about the devotion of the husband and wife to each other, "till death do us part"; but these vows do not mention children.

Nevertheless, having and raising children is a worthy and noble derivative purpose for a romantic, married couple under appropriate circumstances. For many rational individuals, having and raising children (along with grandchildren and great-grandchildren) is the crowning achievement and greatest source of enjoyment of a lifetime.

It is one more example of the integration of the human organism that procreation follows from the intimate bonding of coitus, which in turn is the deepest physical expression of romantic love. Moreover, the matter of children is a very important part of the strictly legal aspect of marriage, as will be discussed below.

Marriage recognizes that an exclusive and permanent romantic relationship is objective evidence for a constellation of effects including these:

- that the relationship is worthy of taking legal precedence over each individual's original family bonds;

– that a child born to the mother is reasonably presumed to have been fathered by her husband (see, for example, Ohio Revised Code Title XXXI, Section 3111.03 "Presumption of paternity"), and that the couple is reasonably presumed committed to raising such a child.

These effects are important aspects of the concept of marriage even though some married couples do not take advantage of one or another of these effects, as the right to vote is an important aspect of citizenship even though some citizens do not avail themselves of that right.

Many kinds of sexual relationships other than marriage are possible. It should go without saying that adults have the right to engage in any sexual act by mutual consent. Why, then, is government involved in marriage more than other kinds of sexual relationships?

Some advocates of limited government argue that government should get out of the marriage business, that marriage is a matter for private contract. But government is implicitly involved in all contracts. Implicit in any contract is that the government will enforce the contract if called on to do so. A marriage ceremony enables the government officially to validate the documents of the marriage contract, which are accompanied by public oaths by the contracting parties, thereby diminishing the possibility that meddlers might challenge the documents in the future.

As Mazlish (2013) explains,

> Mere contractual documents ... can later be challenged. Because they are simply private pieces of paper that can be forged, by their nature they cannot have the same legal presumptions as those that attach to a government officiated marriage.
>
> ...
>
> Without the conclusive presumptions that attach upon a marriage ceremony, persons who rely on mere written contract documents such as powers of attorney,

health care directives and wills have not extinguished
or cut off the rights of disgruntled family members to
challenge the authenticity of those documents.

In many states, homosexuals did not have such a means, afforded
by marriage, to initiate a legal proceeding for designating next of kin.
Every citizen, regardless of his sexual orientation, should have such
a means available to him. Such a proceeding is a legitimate perfection
of individual rights that government should support. But homosexuals are not the only ones who did not have such a legal means available. As a heterosexual bachelor, I too should have the right to a legal
ceremony whereby I can select my best friend, a married heterosexual man, as my next of kin, without my having to have sex with him.
Furthermore, my selecting my best friend as my next of kin should
not mean that I have "married" him.

In my judgment, moreover, establishing next of kin is not the
most compelling reason for government to sanction marriages. The
most compelling reason is to afford an important means for the married couple to protect individual rights pertaining to their conceiving
of children. That is, although the bearing of children is not the most
important aspect of marriage, individual rights pertaining to the
bearing of children is the most important—and most distinctive—
legal aspect of marriage.

A government-witnessed marriage ceremony provides the legal
presumption that the husband is the natural father of any child sub-
sequently born of the wife. This presumption protects the husband,
the wife, and the child from paternity challenges by other men.
Moreover, this presumption protects the mother and child from
abandonment or denial of paternity by the father; stated more posi-
tively, the wedding ceremony affords the husband the opportunity
to make a legally witnessed public pledge that he will be the man responsible for the care of the children born of his wife.

Rights related to adoption of children are a different matter. In
such cases, the child is already born and already has a legal

custodian—even if that custodian is the government—looking out for the child's rights. That legal custodian has means other than marriage to obtain legal presumptions regarding the commitments of the adoptive parent or parents.

The marriage-based legal presumptions pertaining to the individual rights related to the bearing of children apply only to heterosexual couples, of course. Thus, even in the narrow context of legal presumptions made available by government sanction, a marriage is significantly different from other kinds of civil unions.

The concept of marriage, however, is not merely a legal concept. Just as much if not more so, marriage is a moral and romantic concept. Indeed, if government got out of the business of officiating at marriage ceremonies and even sanctioning marriages, the concept of marriage would remain. Private organizations would continue to sanction marriages, just as private organizations sanction accreditations, certifications, graduations, Bar Mitzvahs, and so on.

The basic question regarding the concept of marriage, therefore, is not legal or political, but rather epistemological: Would broadening the concept "marriage," to subsume all legally sanctioned relationships entailing the sharing of property and assigning of next of kin, serve cognition or hinder cognition? If two men mutually pledge to be each other's life partner, does clear cognition demand that the relationship be called a marriage, or a civil union, or some other word?

In my judgment, such a civil union absolutely should not be called a marriage.

I support the traditional concept of marriage, as I defined it at the start of this chapter, not because it is traditional, but because the concept serves an essential cognitive need.

According to the theory of heterosexual romantic love that I have presented—see especially Chapter 1—the role of the man and of the woman in a heterosexual romantic relationship differs profoundly; this difference of course carries through to the relationship of marriage. Let me recapitulate just some of this difference from the perspective of the man. The man knows that he is the physically more powerful partner, that it is his particular responsibility—and joy—to provide physical safety for his wife, to take the lead in actions dealing with survival, to take the lead romantically, and to be in charge sexually. Integrated with these differences are differences in physical appearance, and the man celebrates the woman's sex-specific, feminine beauty acting on all of his senses. For his romantic partner, the man seeks someone who is organized physically to receive his power and thrive on it, within the safe environment he has created for her, and who will judge his efficacy. He seeks a mind equal in stature to his own, who expects him to lead, not merely so that she may follow, but so that she may judge, and so that she may offer her beauty to him alone as the expression of her judgment.

Individuals may reasonably disagree regarding specifics of the sex-related differences between the man and the woman in a rational marriage. Nevertheless, there are such differences, and it is rational for an individual's sexual values to be highly sex-specific. To a rational human being, the sex and sexual orientation of one's spouse is important, to say the least. The concept of marriage must continue to capture that importance, identifying sex and sexual orientation with emphasis and definite clarity.

(Applying the key idea of "measurement omission" from Ayn Rand's theory of concepts—see Ayn Rand ([1966–1967] 1990, 11–18—my point can be restated as follows: Sex cannot be an omitted measurement in a heterosexual's concept of marriage.)

A married man, or a man who desires marriage, needs to know that being married means being a man to a woman, not merely being a partner to a partner. The concept of "marriage" helps him to hold that knowledge in condensed form. This knowledge serves both as a guide to action and a means of contemplating one's romantic success.

The fundamental purpose of incorporating the concepts of "man" and "woman" in the concept of "marriage" is not to distinguish heterosexual relationships from homosexual ones; the fundamental purpose is to enable heterosexuals—and anyone who wants to understand them—to retain, in condensed form, the fact that there are essential differences between men and women. That is why the concept of marriage refers to man and woman without any consideration of homosexuals. If there were no homosexuals, heterosexuals would still need the concept of marriage as identifying a man and a woman as the two parties involved. That is why Ayn Rand's ([1966–1967] 1990, 36) description of marriage explicitly refers to "a man and a woman," even though her discussion of the concept does not address sexual orientation.

If homosexual unions were to be called "marriages," then there would no longer be a word for the current concept of "marriage"; that is, the current concept of marriage would cease to exist. (Since the *Obergefell* decision, many if not most people now consider homosexual unions marriages, but I do not.) But marriage is too exalted an idea not to be a concept. There is even a distinct word for the basic sexual act that is distinct to the joining of a man and woman: coitus. (In fact, there are two such words: coitus and copulation.) It would be bizarrely anti-romantic to have a word for the one exclusively heterosexual sexual act and no word for the most exalted exclusively heterosexual romantic bond.

A heterosexual man should not have to think or say, "I am in a heterosexual marriage" instead of thinking or saying simply, "I am married." The issue is not merely the saving of time in pronouncing words. The issue is good cognition. The phrase "a heterosexual marriage" places far too much emphasis on the distinction between heterosexuals and homosexuals, and buries the romantic distinction between a man and a woman. The phrase removes the romanticism from the concept of marriage.

Similarly, a married man should not have to think or say, "I am married ... to a woman"; and a single man should not have to think, "I desire to be married ... to a woman." These phrases emphasize the distinction between the man being married to a woman vs. his being married to a man. This distinction certainly is not the one that a man wants to have brought to the forefront of his mind when he is contemplating his marriage. One distinction he *does* want brought to the forefront of his mind is the distinction between his feminine wife and his masculine self. The other distinction he wants brought to the forefront of his mind is the distinction between marriage and other, less serious or committed kinds of relationships between a man and a woman. The sentence "I am married" emphasizes these very distinctions, summoning to the mind of the man his understanding of a man's relation to the woman he shares his life with.

Broadening the concept of marriage to include homosexuals would be a killer of conceptual understanding of romantic love, and a killer of romance.

Calling homosexual unions "marriages" is as absurd as calling all spouses "wives." That observation leads to my next point.

If the concept of marriage were extended to include same-sex civil unions, then the concepts of husband and wife also would lose their current sex-specific meanings. Would a man married to a man be a wife, in virtue of his being married to a man, or would he be a husband in virtue of his being a married man, or would he be both? The only way to be unambiguous would be to employ an awkward and difficult-to-grasp phrase such as "a woman married to a man" or "a female spouse of a male spouse" to refer to what we now know as a wife.

The phrase "a woman married to a man" would emphasize the distinction from "a woman married to a woman" or a "a man married to a man"; that is, the phrase would emphasize the distinction between heterosexuals and homosexuals, and bury the distinction between a husband and a wife in a marriage. The phrase "a female spouse of a male spouse" would be even worse. (I analyze this phrase in Appendix 3.) In short, not only would we be left with awkward and confusing phrases in place of "husband" and "wife," but the meaning of "husband" and "wife" would be perverted, stripped of romanticism.

My analysis, above, of the phrases "heterosexual marriage" and "a woman married to a man" is analogous to a philosophical principle familiar to students of Ayn Rand's philosophy of Objectivism: A concept does not mean its definition. (For one analysis of this principle, see Peikoff 1990, 88–106. For my own analysis, which contains significant differences from Peikoff's, see Appendix 3.) The phrase "rational animal" *defines* the concept "man," but the phrase does not capture the full and precise *meaning* of the concept "man." Similarly, the phrase "heterosexual marriage" would not capture the full and precise meaning of the concept "marriage," and the phrase "a woman married to a man" certainly would not capture the full and precise meaning of the concept "wife." These concepts would be lost.

The substitution of "rational animal" for "man," however, is not nearly as bad as the substitution of "heterosexual marriage" for the conception of marriage, or the substitution of "a woman married to a man" or, equivalently, "a heterosexual married woman" for "wife." The reason is that at least "rational animal" is a good definition of "man"; "rational" is a good distinguishing characteristic of "man," a good distinction of "man" to emphasize. But "heterosexual" is not a good distinction to emphasize as a characteristic of the conceptions of "marriage" or "wife."

The very existence of the concepts "husband" and "wife," let alone the prevalence in usage of these concepts over the concept "spouse," is strong corroborating evidence for the conclusion that we need to retain the concept "marriage" in its traditional form. Further corroborating evidence is that we use the concepts "mother" and "father" more than "parent," and the concepts "brother" and "sister" even than "sibling." We also have the concepts "bride" and "groom," not merely "newlywed," and "son" and "daughter," not merely "off-spring." For certain important concepts, sex matters.

Even among advocates for homosexuality, the overwhelmingly predominant view is to insist on separate words for male homosex-ual ("gay") and female homosexual ('lesbian'); hence the "L" and "G" in "LGBT'. Moreover, leading pro-homosexual researchers often in-sist that statistical data on one homosexual "gender" (such as high percentages of promiscuous male homosexuals) differ from data on the other "gender." (See, for example, Peplau 2003.) Even to advo-cates for homosexuality, sex matters in concepts.

In a heterosexual relationship, unlike a homosexual one, there is a difference in sex between the two partners, and this difference is fundamental. The romantic concepts of a heterosexual are awash in the recognition and celebration of the difference between man and woman, between masculinity and femininity. To a heterosexual, a husband is not merely one of the two partners in a loving relation-ship; a husband is a masculine man united with a feminine woman. This union between husband and wife is marriage.

For those who want to change the meaning of a concept in the free marketplace of ideas, they are free to try to change one mind at a time through persuasion; and the burden of proof is on them. In my judgment as explained above, this burden regarding "marriage" cannot be met. Instead, advocates of same-sex unions should coin a word or phrase distinct from "marriage." (Or they should coin one word for male couples and another word for female couples, as they always insist on distinguishing between "gays" and "lesbians.") A word might also be coined to subsume both "marriage" and "same-sex union" (or some single word for "same-sex union"), as "spouse" subsumes "husband" and "wife," and as "parent" subsumes "mother" and "father." But we must not lose the current concept "marriage," as we must not lose the concepts "husband" and "wife" or "mother" and "father."

What is doubly wrong is for government—the agency of force—
to change the meaning of a fundamental, rational concept by legal
decree.

The notion of "homosexual marriage," or "same-sex marriage,"
is at best an offensive metaphor corrupting the exalted, sex-specific
aspects of an exalted concept. More often, however, this notion is
also an attempt to seek the unearned.

Marriage is, in principle and despite all the awful marriages that
we all know exist, a profoundly good relationship: for the husband
and wife, and for children that the husband and wife raise or otherwise interact with. The notion of "same-sex marriage" implies the
premise that a homosexual union is as good as marriage for all involved. To say the least, the present book challenges this premise; but
more politically significant than my challenge is this point: It is not
the business of government to end the debate over this premise by
fiat, by declaring new meanings for a fundamental, rational concept
in a free society.

The attempt by LGBT activists to end this debate, by changing the
meaning of an essential concept, is another attempt to prevent individuals from judging them. The LGBT activists are seeking an unearned legitimacy by riding on the established reputation of marriage. Though LGBT activists deride their opponents for being con-
strained by tradition, it is the LGBT activists who want to cash in on
the tradition of others. As LGBT activists have gotten their way, they
have pushed for further action by government to forbid private
adoption agencies from discriminating between heterosexual and
same-sex couples. (See Anderson 2015, 87–91. All such couples, after
all, are now deemed "married.") The activists have also pushed for
more indoctrination in government schools, claiming that all "marriages" are equal. (See Pullmann 2019.) Ultimately, the activists will
push for the eradication of all sex-specific words, including "mother"
and "father," "husband" and "wife," and "masculine" and "feminine." By eradicating crucial, sex-specific words, the LGBT activists

seek to eradicate the ability of individuals to hold sex-specific concepts and have sex-specific thoughts—except, hypocritically, to distinguish "gays" from "lesbians."

If recent actions by government regarding the word "marriage"
show anything, it is that government is not a reliable defender of
such an important word. The word "marriage" has a long history
both within government and outside of government, and the very
meaning of the word contains both legal and romantic characteristics. In today's culture, it is important to protect the word both from
non-heterosexual activists *and* government. A case might be made
that government should abdicate the word completely, leaving its use
to be determined solely by individuals privately, and that government should adopt the term "civil union" for all civil unions. After
all, I do not care whether homosexuals think and say that they are
married, as long as I know that only heterosexual couples are married, and that I remain politically free to use the English language
accordingly.

But government abdicating the word "marriage" opens the door
to other frivolous demands that government abdicate other words,
such as "man" and "woman." Moreover, as argued above, the most
important role of government pertaining to marriage is in protecting
rights pertaining to a married couple's children, and this role applies
only to heterosexual, married couples. Therefore, government
should continue to use the word "marriage," and should retain the
traditional legal meaning of the concept.

There is one other government policy to insist upon to protect
the word "marriage": federalism. The legal definition of marriage
should be kept away from the federal government, and left in the
hands of state or local governments. That way, states with more rational citizens would not be affected by the decisions in states with
less rational citizens. At the same time, same-sex couples who want
to get "married" could move to the less rational states.

In summary, words represent concepts. Some words are worth fighting for. "Marriage," denoting a crucial kind of relationship between a man and a woman, is such a word.

CONCLUSION

This conclusion re-emphasizes important points from the book, and expands on thematic points from the Introduction.

Masculine Power, Feminine Beauty

Chapter 1 presented my theory of heterosexuality. I argued that heterosexuality in particular enables romantic love in a way that integrates with all aspects of a man and woman. In a heterosexual romantic relationship, the man and the woman each make choices that leverage their biological advantages—the man's physical power and the woman's physical beauty—in such a way as to celebrate each individual's efficacy in a benevolent universe. In Chapter 6, I argued that good cognition requires that the most exalted kind of romantic relationship between a man and a woman be conceptualized with a single word: "marriage."

In short, understanding the implications of masculine power and feminine beauty forms the objective basis for heterosexuality in romantic love and marriage.

My theory is based on my introspection, personal observations of myself and others, and contemplation of heroes and heroines in Romantic fiction. I deliberately omitted any advanced science to support my theory. The evidence for my theory should be available to anyone—even a child—who has lived in Western civilization and had an opportunity to observe adult men and women.

According to my own personal conception of masculinity, masculine sexuality is an expression of my power and efficacy. My power is under the direction of my reasoning mind that knows what to do to command nature and thrive. For a romantic partner, I seek someone who is organized physically to receive my power and thrive on it, within the safe environment I have created for her, and who will judge my efficacy. I seek a mind equal in stature to my own, who expects me to lead, not merely so that she may follow, but so that she may judge, and so that she may offer her beauty to me alone as the expression of her judgment.

According to my own personal conception of marriage, the husband has the responsibility—and joy—to provide physical safety for his wife, to take the lead in urgent actions dealing with survival, to be the primary source of physical power as a complement to his wife's beauty, to take the lead romantically, and to be in charge sexually. That is, it is the husband's responsibility and joy to be masculine, and to enjoy the femininity of his wife.

Consistent with my ideas on masculinity, femininity, romantic love, and marriage are my attractions. I find a virtuous, beautiful woman sexually appealing, and I am violently repulsed by the thought of sexual relations with a man.

My conceptions of masculinity and femininity are not merely a matter of personal preference; they are objective, based on factual, physical differences between men and women. Other heterosexual men and women may differ with me on details of masculinity, femininity, romantic love, and marriage while recognizing the physical difference between men and women; there is room for personal preference within objectivity. (In Appendices 4 and 5, other individuals offer their own conceptions of masculinity and femininity.) But for all of us, the difference between man and woman—as we perceive, conceive, and respond emotionally to this difference—is crucial to our romantic relationship. As the saying goes, "Vive la différence!"

A person's sex is important. To a married man, it is important that his spouse is a woman, not a man. That is, it is important that his spouse is a wife. To a homosexual man, it is important that the person he has sexual relations with is a man, not a woman. To people in the LGBT movement, it is important to distinguish male homosexuals (denoted by the "G" for "Gay") from female homosexuals (denoted by the "L" for "Lesbian"). To "transgenders," sex is so important that many of them are willing to mutilate their genitals in order to "transition" to the other sex, the sex they would rather be.

Sex is so important that we have the words "man" and "woman," not merely "person"; "husband" and "wife," not merely "spouse"; "bride" and "groom," not merely "newlywed." We even have the words "mother" and "father," not merely "parent"; "son" and "daughter," not merely "offspring"; "brother" and "sister," not merely "sibling." For the same reason—only more so—that we need these other sex-specific words, we need a word for the most exalted bond specifically between a man and a woman. That word is "marriage."

Let there be a word for a bond between two men. Let there be another word for a bond between two women. Let there be a term— "civil union"—for all such bonds. But we must never lose the word for the most crucial kind of bond between a man and a woman. Sex is important.

Since *Obergefell*, the United States government's new, impoverished, sexless notion of marriage may suffice for a homosexual, for whom there is no difference in sex between himself and his partner. But the new notion, by de-emphasizing what is fundamental, destroys the concepts of husband, wife, and marriage for heterosexuals. The government has—by decree—neutered and homogenized the most romantic concepts, for heterosexuals, in the English language. And that is the fundamental reason why government-sanctioned same-sex marriage is so terribly wrong.

Two men have a right to say that they are married. And I have a right to say that they are not. I have a right to use, in my own mind and in my communication and trade with others, the concept of marriage exclusively for unions between man and woman. Moreover, this sex-specific conception of marriage is the more rational one, the one more conducive to clear cognition and romantic fulfillment.

Government is wrong to use the force of law to undercut and pervert this rational romantic concept.

The Role of Volition

In my judgment after considering the mainstream theories of etiology, and as argued in Chapters 2 and 3, a person's sex-specific sexual values are caused ultimately by his ideas. Ideas are not assessed appropriately by terms such as "illness." Ideas are true or false, right or wrong. The value of a particular individual's sex-specific sexual evaluation depends on the truth or falsehood of the ideas that underlie it. In particular, the value of my sex-specific sexual evaluation—heterosexuality, as I understand heterosexuality—depends on the truth or falsehood of the ideas presented for it in Chapter 1.

All ideas are formed through a volitional process. However, as explained in Chapter 2,

> the choices that set an individual's sex-specific sexual evaluations might be made when the individual is very young. Tragically, a child may have little way of knowing that seemingly small choices can be important, that such choices when added together can shape his entire view of the world and his place in it. An individual should not be condemned, and perhaps not even criticized, for such early choices.

Generally, an individual does not directly choose his sex-specific sexual evaluation, but—as with other aspects of his sense of life—he makes other choices that ultimately lead to this evaluation. It is often inappropriate to characterize such early choices as moral or immoral, but such early choices either are right or wrong, correct or mistaken, beneficial to life or harmful to it.

That choices leading to homosexuality are made by innocent children has another implication. Adults can convey misinformation and expose children to a skewed set of experiences, forming a basis upon which children might make misinformed evaluations that lead to homosexuality.

Therefore, all individuals should be free to choose to limit their own—and especially their children's—interaction with homosexuals or any individuals who embrace the ideas of the LGBT movement.

Sexual Nihilism of the LGBT Movement

Chapter 4 examined the mainstream theories of the etiology of sexual orientation and found only theories of determinism and subjectivism masquerading as science. This masquerade consists of studying and measuring all kinds of things except what needs to be studied: the reasoning mind of man. The shared premise of all these theories is the notion that sexual orientation is mindless because sexuality is mindless. The result of all these theories is a foul wasteland of sexual nihilism.

Chapter 5 showed that the nihilism of the LGBT movement extends beyond the subject of sexuality and encompasses all Western values, including reason, productiveness, independence, and capitalism.

But many non-heterosexuals *are not* part of the LGBT movement (and many heterosexuals *are* part of the movement). Many non-heterosexuals are far better than the LGBT activists. Many non-heterosexuals are ethical, share basic values with their partner, are loving and monogamous, and are not out to destroy Western civilization. But many good non-heterosexuals, as well as good heterosexuals, have been hoodwinked by the LGBT activists who claim that facts and science are on the side of the LGBT activists regarding the subject of sexual orientation. Chapters 4 and 5, along with some of Chapter 3, debunk that claim.

Good, decent non-heterosexuals need to distance themselves from and disavow the nihilist ideas of the LGBT movement—for the sake of themselves and any children they might interact with.

The Need for Theory

Some civilized and reasonable defenders of non-heterosexuality argue that they have homosexual friends who are exemplars of reason, morality, and love that is based on rational values. They are right. But friends—even closest friends—are rarely if ever in a position to attest to the quality of one another's sex life.

If a couple is ethical, shares basic values, and is loving and monogamous, these factors will be all to the good and will yield great benefits. But these factors do not imply that the couple's sex-specific sexual evaluation is to the good as well. Good people who are right about many things, even fundamental things, can yet be mistaken about other important things. Being right in some respects does not imply being right in all respects. To argue that a couple's sex-specific sexual values are good based on the premise that the individuals are good people is to make an appeal to authority.

Sexual orientation is not an immaterial issue such as race. Race is a passive attribute. An individual's race, in comparison to other races, does not imply any meaningfully different actions by that individual. But an individual's sexual orientation implies very different actions from those based on other sexual orientations. Unless an individual is bisexual, his sexual orientation implies that he acts to discriminate and exclude an entire sex in favor of the other sex in regard to a crucial matter, the matter of sexual relations. Such crucial actions call for rational explanation. What is needed is not a claim that good people are of a certain sexual orientation. What is needed is a *theory* of sex-specific sexual evaluation. In Chapter 1, I offered my theory.

If any LGBT activists read my theory, they will probably attack it—and offer no objective theory in response. The LGBT movement thrives on sophistry, attacking all theories and defending only skepticism and abject subjectivism. The LGBT activists conclude that anything goes because, after all, they are not sick. The movement thrives in particular on the erection and destruction of intrinsicist straw-man arguments such as arguments based on religion and tradition.

Attacking the sexual orientation of religious zealots, or attacking my sexual orientation, does not bring anyone closer to understanding his own.

Understand Your Sex-Specific Sexual Evaluation

Now we arrive again at the overarching theme of this book. Whatever one thinks about the relative merits of various sex-specific sexual values, *it is better to understand the ideas underlying one's sex-specific sexual evaluation than not to understand them.*

The more we understand why we are moved by a certain work of art or kind of art, the deeper we will be moved, and the deeper will be our love for the art. As in art, so in romance.

As a heterosexual, I am most interested in understanding more about heterosexuality. I want to learn more about how romantic love—and the relationship of marriage especially—integrates with all aspects of being a man and being a woman. I want to learn more about the ideas and objective, sex-specific values that underlie such a relationship.

Of all the hoodwinking perpetrated by the LGBT movement, the worst has been to hoodwink decent people into believing that there are no important ideas underlying their sexual orientation. But there are.

I return to the good-will challenge—to those of any sexual orientation—that I offered in the Introduction: I can explain how my sexual orientation is consistent with my other basic values; can you do the same for yours?

I am not suggesting that anyone perform psychoanalysis on himself. Even if you do not think that you can uncover the ideas that initially led you to your sex-specific sexual values, and even if you think that your sex-specific sexual evaluation will not change, then I ask, "What conscious ideas do you now hold that are consistent with the fact that you are sexually attracted to this one sex and not the other (or, if you are bisexual, to both sexes)?" If you truly believe that your current sexual orientation is good for you, then you should believe that knowing the answer to this question will do you great further good.

Moreover, if you truly believe that a certain sexual orientation would be good for a child, then you should believe that the child knowing why would do him great further good.

I close with a repetition of this quotation of Ayn Rand ([1966] 1975, 33):

> Love is *the expression of philosophy*—of a subconscious philosophical sum—and, perhaps, no other aspect of human existence needs the *conscious* power of philosophy quite so desperately. When that power is called upon to verify and support an emotional appraisal, when love is a conscious integration of reason and emotion, of mind and values, then—and only then—it is the greatest reward of man's life.

Appendix 1: It Takes Two and No More Than Two

Polygamy and polyamory are such absurd notions, in this day and age informed by the individualism of the Enlightenment, that I will devote only one page to these notions.

Having two romantic partners instead of one is not merely not as good because of less time available for each partner. Such an arrangement is a total failure—much worse than having no one. Such an arrangement is indeed having no one, combined with the acceptance than each person is not good enough for anyone.

Moreover, no second best romantic partner can substitute for the best, but is instead a betrayal of the highest values of the man and woman.

A sexual threesome is an absurdity. It is like presenting your life's work to two people who are paying attention only half the time each. That is worse than presenting to an empty room. As the number of participants increases, the situation becomes even more anonymous and self-abasing. Such a gathering provides physical sensations with spiritual anonymity.

A multi-partner "romance" follows the same pattern. A true romantic partner is a constant primary spiritual companion, even when the partners are apart. With multiple partners, there is no such constancy. Plus, there is this realization: none of us is good enough on our own to be such a constant companion.

APPENDIX 2: TRANSGENDERISM

Several recent books and articles express common sense, backed by evidence, in opposition to the transgender craze. (See, for example, Littman 2018 and Evans and Evans 2021. See Kay 2019 for attempts by transgender activists to suppress Littman's research. See also Anderson 2019, banned by Amazon, and Shrier 2020, banned by Target.) The following brief discussion identifies the fundamental of the matter.

The "Medical Clinical Policy Bulletin" on "Gender Affirming Surgery" published by the Aetna (2021) insurance company, states the following:

> Aetna considers gender affirming surgery medically necessary when all of the following criteria are met:
>
> I. Requirements for breast removal:
>
> A. Single letter of referral from a qualified mental health professional (see Appendix); and
>
> B. Persistent, well-documented gender dysphoria (see Appendix); and
>
> C. Capacity to make a fully informed decision and to consent for treatment; and
>
> D. For members less than 18 years of age, completion of one year of testosterone treatment; and
>
> E. If significant medical or mental health concerns are present, they must be reasonably well controlled.

The document specifies similar "requirements" for "breast augmentation," "gonadectomy," and "genital reconstructive surgery." The afore-referenced Appendix states the following:

DSM 5 Criteria for Gender Dysphoria in Adults and Adolescents

I. A marked incongruence between one's experienced/expressed gender and assigned gender, of at least 6 months duration, as manifested by two or more of the following:

A. A marked incongruence between one's experienced/expressed gender and primary and/or secondary sex characteristics (or, in young adolescents, the anticipated secondary sex characteristics)

B. A strong desire to be rid of one's primary and/or secondary sex characteristics because of a marked incongruence with one's experienced/expressed gender (or, in young adolescents, a desire to prevent the development of the anticipated secondary sex characteristics)

C. A strong desire for the primary and/or secondary sex characteristics of the other gender

D. A strong desire to be of the other gender (or some alternative gender different from one's assigned gender)

E. A strong desire to be treated as the other gender (or some alternative gender different from one's assigned gender)

F. A strong conviction that one has the typical feelings and reactions of the other gender (or some

alternative gender different from one's assigned
gender)

II. The condition is associated with clinically significant
distress or impairment in social, occupational, or
other important areas of functioning.

Observe that the essential requirement for this major insurance
company to pay for irreversible surgical alteration of sex organs is "a
strong desire" that persists for six months. There is no requirement
for any kind of objective, scientific evidence—no genetic evidence,
no physical evidence of any kind—that the individual is anything
other than his obvious biological sex. Other major insurance companies Anthem(2021), Cigna (2021), and Humana (2021) have similar policies (although the required duration of gender dysphoria
may vary to as much as two years instead of six months).

Everyone who has ever been a parent or child knows that many,
if not most, if not all, children experience uncertainty or fear about
being a worthy and desirable exemplar of their biological sex. It is
very common for a child to feel the desire to escape the fundamental
human test of being worthy of one's sex. Most children ultimately
face their fear, recast their fear as excitement, and embrace their im-
mutable identity as a man or woman. Transgenderism is a pandering
to the fear, offering ignorant children a false escape from their im-
mutable sexuality, feeding them a lifelong course of chemicals that
put their body at war with itself, mutilating their sex organs, turning
potential men and women into disintegrated monstrosities.

As with homosexuality, I am using stern language—for the same
reason. It is one thing for an adult to mutilate his own body (using
his own money, not socialized medicine). But to mutilate the body
of a child? No language can be stern enough.

Evens and Evans 2021 would be worth quoting in its entirety, but
here is one particularly poignant passage:

Moreover, in our experience, we have found that children wishing to transition subconsciously often hope that a parental figure will step in and help to identify and understand the part of the self that they are trying to discard. Some detransitioners mention, after the fact, that they were disappointed by doctors' and therapists' inability to stand up to their insistent demands for transition action.

The Human Rights Campaign is an organization that describes itself as "Leading the fight for LGBTQ rights." It's corporate "Platinum Partners" include American Airlines, Apple, Intel, Microsoft, Target, and UPS (https://www.hrc.org/about/corporate-partners). The organization's website defines "cisgender" as follows:

Cisgender | A term used to describe a person whose gender identity aligns with those typically associated with the sex assigned to them at birth. (https://www.hrc.org/resources/glossary-of-terms)

Note the phrase, "assigned to them at birth." This phrase implies a status that is distinct from something identified as true or real. This thinking goes beyond "a strong desire" to be the opposite sex. The transgender people claim that they actually *are* the opposite sex. (This claim often is mediated by an invented term, "gender," that is used as a surrogate for sex.) As the Aetna bulletin illustrates, this claim is based on feelings—not fact, not science, not reasoning.

But no one *feels* that he is a man, and no one *feels* that he is a woman. A man *knows* that he is a man, as a boy knows that he is a boy, by a combination of perceptual observation and conceptual thought. A boy observes perceptual differences between men and women, boys and girls, and thereby forms the concepts "man," "woman," "boy," and "girl." A boy also perceives physical characteristics of himself, and conceptually identifies himself as a boy who will grow into a man.

A man may feel emotions *about* his being a man, or *about* his not being a woman. For instance, he may feel happy that he is a man, or he may feel fear about being a man; or he may feel a *desire* to be a woman, or he may feel a kind of comfort or relief or excitement when *imagining* that he were a woman. But no man can feel *that* he is a woman, or a man, or anything else for that matter. Emotions are responses, not identifications. A man's claim that he feels that he is a woman is a claim of revelation: it is a claim that some consciousness other than his own has attached an identification to his emotion.

To see a clear example of this mystical form of thinking, consider this pair of statements made by Bruce Jenner to Diane Sawyer during the famous 2015 interview (Sawyer 2015) in which Jenner claimed that he is a woman. Early in the interview, Jenner states,

> My brain is much more female than it is male. It is hard for people to understand that, but that is what my soul is.
>
> …
>
> It's just the way I am, the way I was born.

Later in the interview, Jenner states,

> I had this feeling, kind of a revelation, that maybe this is my cause in life. This is why God put me on this Earth, to deal with this issue. That was a very powerful moment. It certainly gave me a lot of courage.

The epistemological status of these two statements by Jenner is the same. Both statements are claims of mystical revelation based on feelings.

To understand the ruining of young lives by the transgender movement, consider this dialogue, from the same television episode (Sawyer 2015), between Sawyer and Dr. Johanna Olson, MD, "of Children's Hospital, Los Angeles, a pediatrician who now directs the

largest treatment program for transgender youth in the country."
(Olson is now Olson-Kennedy, having "married" a transgender individual.) Sawyer is asking Olson to explain how (quoting Sawyer)
"thousands and thousands of people know with certainty that their
real gender is not the same as their anatomy."

Sawyer: You say, born this way.

Olson: Yes. Just made this way. Made this way.

Cut to a video with Sawyer's voiceover: And Dr. Olson
says above all, being transgender is not a mental illness.
…

Olson: Genitals don't equal gender.

Sawyer (voiceover): Our gender, she believes, is not really what we're seeing in the mirror.

Olson: More and more, we're looking at [the theory
that] it lives in the brain.

Cut to a graphic with Sawyer's voiceover explaining Olson's theory: … parts of the brain somehow receive different [hormonal] information than the rest of the
body.

Olson: The youngest kid that I have ever heard talking
about their gender is eighteen months.
…

Sawyer: What kind of word can you use at eighteen
months for this?

Dr. Olson: "I a boy."

Children think conceptually when they are eighteen months old.
That is how they are able to speak words and simple sentences. But
neither conceptual knowledge nor values nor emotional evaluations
are deposited into a passive mind by hormones. A human mind—at

every age, including at eighteen months—makes conceptual identifications and conceptual evaluations by acts of volition. Furthermore, such conceptualizations can be *mistaken*, or even absurd.

This assumption—that a girl can have passively-acquired, not-to-
be questioned, highly abstract conceptual knowledge that she is
somehow a boy—is as mystical as believing that the child is the mes-
siah.

Many of the "thousands and thousands of people" who allegedly
"know with certainty that their real gender is not the same as their
anatomy" are children who have been reassigned to the opposite sex
based on thoughts and feelings described by the children themselves.

Transgender activists claim that "gender," or what is rationally
understood as sex, "lives in the brain," that individuals are born with
a brain that is either male or female. But what does such a notion
mean? Consider these questions:

– What are the criteria for classifying a brain as male or female, or
  some combination of the two, at birth?
– How does the sex of the brain affect its functioning?
– How does the sex of the brain affect the thoughts, values, and emotions that the mind will eventually have?
– Do these affected emotions include sexual orientation? If not, why
  is this particular category of emotions not affected?
– How does the sex of the brain affect a person's epistemology?
– How does having a penis, and not a vagina, impair the mental
  functioning of a man with a female brain?
– How does slicing his penis and reshaping it into a dysfunctional
  vagina, along with making other physical changes such as taking
  female hormones, improve the mental functioning of a man with
  a female brain?

There are no reasonable answers to these questions that are consistent with transgenderism. Knowledge of one's sex, like all human
knowledge, comes from perceptual experience and conceptualization of that experience, not by innate ideas, and not by mystically

intuiting the sex of one's brain. Individual abilities to perceive and conceptualize differ in degree, and undoubtedly differ in degree by sex (at least roughly). But whatever the degree of these abilities, any reasoning mind can make the most of—instead of rejecting—one's physical endowments.

And remember, children are having their genitals mutilated without first having their brains tested somehow for physical maleness or femaleness. The children merely express "a strong desire" lasting six months. This notion of male and female brains is a red herring.

The basis of transgenderism is not science or medicine. The basis is Leftist ideology. Recall the words, quoted at greater length in Chapter 5, from R.W. Connell (1987, 277), a transgender professor with more than 95,000 citations on Google Scholar:

Connell, 1987, 183:

> There is an ordering of versions of femininity and masculinity at the level of the whole society ... Their interrelation is centered on a single structural fact, the global dominance of men over women.

Connell, 1987, 287:

> If the abolition of gender is a worthwhile goal, then it must be the abolition of gender as a social structure that is at issue. ... Difference between sexes would be simply a complementarity of function in reproduction, not a cosmic division or a social fate. There would be no reason for this to structure emotional relationships, so the categories heterosexual and homosexual would become insignificant. There would be no reason for it to structure character, so femininity and masculinity would depart.

Connell 1987, 288:

> The logical consequence of deconstruction is open-
> ended variety. Marcuse's discussion of 'polymorphous
> perversity' in *Eros and Civilization* is not a bad sum-
> mary of this conception, though with rules dismantled
> nothing can be defined as normative and hence noth-
> ing as 'perverse'.

Connell 1987, 292:

> As a matter of fact, the core institutions of the contem-
> porary structure of gender power cannot be torn down
> without a class politics, because those institutions fuse
> gender and class domination. As a matter of practice,
> equality is difficult to contain; the origins of modern
> feminist radicalism in the New Left show that. The his-
> toric association between socialism and feminism,
> however tense and ragged it has been, expresses a basic
> truth about the global structure of inequality and what
> social forces might dismantle it.

Transgenderism—the "T" in "LGBT"—lays bare that the LGBT
movement is the most evil ideological movement in the history of
the English-speaking world, because this movement advocates and
practices the purest form of mindless indulgence of emotion—in the
service of destroying Western civilization, poisoning the sexual potential of children, and mutilating their bodies.

APPENDIX 3: WHY A DEFINITION DOES NOT MEAN THE CONCEPT THAT IT DEFINES

A definition does not equal the meaning of a concept; the classic example is that the defining phrase "the rational animal" is not the same as the concept "man." For one analysis of the difference between a definition and the meaning of a concept, see Peikoff 1990, 88–106. My own analysis below has some significant differences.

It is true that the phrase "rational animal" refers to all men (including women) and only to men. It is true that all rational animals are organized to stand upright and move gracefully on two legs, have faces that express their powerful emotions that can be consistent with their rationality, have hands to shape the world in accordance with their rationality, have the capacity to integrate rational values with sexual desire, and are all members of a single species that has a distinctive physical appearance and other distinctive physical characteristics. That is, the phrase "rational animal," once informed with the above knowledge, can identify all the attributes identified by the word "man." But the words "rational" and "animal," taken separately, do not so identify all these attributes.

As Ayn Rand (1990, 66–67) has identified, a concept is (metaphorically) a kind of "file folder" that includes many—open-endedly many—attributes of the referents of the concept. In my judgment, a phrase—such as "rational animal"—can also be such a file folder. However, in my judgment, the content of such a file folder, of either a concept or a phrase, is not a mere list of characteristics. The characteristics within a conceptual file-folder are arranged in a hierarchy. Such a hierarchy is the basis for, among other things, the rule of fundamentality: the most fundamental characteristics of a concept—

such as the characteristics "rational" and "animal" of the concept "man," belong in a concept's definition. (In my "Theory of Propositions," I write at length about the characteristics of a concept being in a hierarchy.) Other characteristics, such as that man can speak language, are derivative of more fundamental characteristics.

And here we arrive at the crux of the issue. Although the phrase "the rational animal" means more than its constituent parts "rational" and "animal"—that is, although the phrase "the rational animal" encompasses all the characteristics encompassed by the concept "man"—the phrase nevertheless encompasses all of these characteristics in a different hierarchy, a different order of importance than the order entailed by the concept "man." The phrase "the rational animal" overly emphasizes the characteristics identified by each word—in particular, the word "animal"—taken separately, in an order of importance relevant to each word taken separately. That is, the phrase "the rational animal" elevates and emphasizes all characteristics of all animals (such as that animals locomote and have a certain kind of cell structure in contrast to plants), and it underemphasizes characteristics beyond rationality and even derived from rationality that are specific to and important to men (such as the characteristics of standing upright, having expressive faces, and having the capacity to integrate reason and emotion). Even on a perceptual level, the phrase "the rational animal" tends to summon to mind the figure of a non-human animal rather than the figure of a man.

From another perspective, the phrase "rational animal" overemphasizes the distinction between men and animals, and it underemphasizes the distinction between men and all other kinds of entities. For instance, I do not have to think of animals to grasp the irreplaceable value of a man compared to the value of a piece of property. You don't begin teaching a child to value human life by explaining that a human being is more valuable than a dog. You say something like, "We can get a new car, but we cannot get a new Johnny." Therefore, the phrase "rational animal" does not do justice as a substitute for the concept "man."

Similarly and even more starkly, the phrase "female spouse of a male spouse" does not do justice to the concept "wife." Beyond being extremely awkward and difficult to hold in one's mind, this phrase overly emphasizes strictly biological features of being female and male (such as having specifically male or female reproductive organs), along with legal and social characteristics of being a spouse, and de-emphasizes the distinctive kind of regard that a rational married woman qua woman has for her rational husband qua man (and vice versa).

From another perspective, the phrase "female spouse of a male spouse" overemphasizes a distinction from "female spouse of a female spouse" and "male spouse of a male spouse," and it underemphasizes the difference between a husband and a wife in a marriage. This problem of emphasis is much worse in the case of "female spouse of a male spouse" than it is in the case of "rational animal." The reason—as I mentioned in Chapter 7—is that "rational animal" is a good definition of "man," but "female spouse of a male spouse" is a bad definition of "wife." Indeed, if the meaning of marriage were broadened to include homosexual couples, then there would be no good definition of "wife" or of "husband" or "marriage" as we now understand these concepts, because "heterosexual" would have to be included among the distinguishing characteristics stated in any definition.

Even the phrase "woman spouse of a man" de-emphasizes essential characteristics of being a wife, characteristics that are not contained in the meaning of the words "woman," "spouse," and "man" considered separately.

APPENDIX 4: BY CHARLOTTE CUSHMAN

FEMININITY, ROMANCE, AND FAMILY

Femininity

The Nature of the Female

The differences between the sexes can be observed at a very early age. As a Montessori teacher for decades, and as a parent, I have seen boys as young as one year of age fascinated with trucks and trains, and girls interested in dolls. Boys tend to be more active and rough than girls, they like to run and tumble, whereas girls are less active and more gentle. Boys are outwardly focused, whereas girls are more inwardly focused (they care about what dress they are wearing). When social problems arise, boys tend to resolve those problems physically, whereas girls try to resolve them with words. Girls try to understand and manage relationships, whereas boys care more about their pursuits in the real world. Yes, there are exceptions, but overall these are the tendencies.

Looking back on my own childhood, I had the same female tendencies. When I was a little girl, I wanted to know what it was really like to take care of a baby, so I pretended that my doll was a real baby. I dressed her, pretended to feed her and change her diaper, cuddled her, protected her, and rocked her to sleep. I liked pretty dresses and especially liked to twirl in them--the farther out the twirl, the more successful the dress. I liked reading the stories of a woman being rescued from evil doers by a man who loved her, and dreamed of being loved by a hero when I grew up.

As I grew older I became a tomboy because I liked to play outside with the boys, but during adolescence this changed. Although I was proud that I could do some challenging feats (like tilt the motor on the boat all by myself), overall, I was not interested in doing the physically demanding activities that the boys were doing. I didn't think those activities were fun, nor was I good at doing them.

I have always liked being a girl, even when I was a tomboy. I love clothes, jewelry, flowers, lace and anything else that accentuates my femininity. The song from *Flower Drum Song* called "I Enjoy Being a Girl" describes me to a "T." Being female is fun.

As an adult I do not like doing the same physical work that my husband enjoys. I much prefer doing laundry, cooking, sewing, and creating a pleasing and beautiful home to shoveling snow, mowing the lawn, stacking wood, or changing the oil in the car. When the children were little, I typically was the one who comforted them, and he was the one who got them to laugh with his tumble play and torture tickles. This isn't to say that we never reversed our roles, or that people shouldn't choose different roles. It's just that those are the roles that we preferred and still prefer.

Being the weaker sex gives me a sense of vulnerability and, therefore, I tend to be more cautious than my husband. I am more concerned about safety rather than taking risks. In crisis situations, I have a tendency to feel more frightened than he does. I think this feeling of vulnerability could explain why, during a crisis, women can have more of a tendency to break down emotionally.

I also am aware of the possibility of rape or sexual assault from dangerous, uncivilized men. I don't walk through life on a day-to-day basis feeling afraid, but any vulnerability that is felt by other women will vary depending on what they have experienced. Men might not be aware of these feelings if women do not share the negative experiences. For me, it was very difficult and took time for me to build up the courage to tell my husband about mine because they are so ugly and unpleasant to talk about.

It is obvious to me that the differences between my husband and me are more than just the anatomical differences. I agree with Ron that there are differences between the sexes based on the choices they make because of the conclusions that they draw about their respective biological makeups. In my judgment, such differences include psychological differences. It makes sense that the physically stronger person would choose to be braver, more aggressive, willing to take more risks, and more inclined toward harder work and rougher play. And it also makes sense that the person physically constructed to bear children would gravitate toward being nurturing, and would favor domestic activities—such as preparing a safe and pleasant home—over physically demanding activities. It is also logical that women tend to focus on relationships more than men do, because in nature they are dependent on men for survival.

The biological makeup of the female body is for the purpose of creating life. This fact presents every female with the choice to bear children. As long as I can remember, I wanted to have children. Although not every woman makes that choice, most do. Speaking for myself, raising a family with a loving husband provided me with personal fulfillment, and the resulting joy that I feel is the hallmark of motherhood.

The State of Being Feminine

I am well aware of men's strength, and I admire it. The strength that I admire in a man is not only his physical strength, but more importantly his intellectual strength because his intellect is what determines the actions he takes. I agree with Ayn Rand (1968, 1–2) when she writes,

> For a woman *qua* woman, the essence of femininity is hero-worship—the desire to look up to man. "To look up" does not mean dependence, obedience or anything implying inferiority. It means an intense kind of admiration; and admiration is an emotion that can be experienced only by a person of strong character and independent value-judgments. A "clinging vine" type of

woman is not an admirer, but an exploiter of men.
Hero-worship is a demanding virtue: a woman has to
be worthy of it and of the hero she worships. Intellectually and morally, i.e., as a human being, she has to be
his equal; then the object of her worship is specifically
his *masculinity*, not any human virtue she might lack.

I love masculine men. Not only have men made the lives of everyone easier by building structures for survival and inventing ma-
chines that make work easier, but men have fought in numerous
wars in order to protect their family and homeland and end the ini-
tiation of violence from thieves, murderers, thugs, communists, and
so on. They have also written beautiful music and poetry expressing
deep and meaningful emotions.

It was men who paved the way for women to be lifted out of sexual discrimination by writing the Declaration of Independence that
proclaimed the idea of equality, and the right to one's own life, liberty, and the pursuit of happiness. It is primarily masculine men who
have built and protected Western civilization, and who have saved
women and children from barbarians such as rapists and thieves.

Masculine men make me feel safe, and I want them to exist for
my safety. I can take care of myself, but when I have been accosted
by predators, I was very glad and appreciative to have a moral, masculine man nearby who stepped in and helped me. The fact of the
matter is I do not have the same physical strength as a man. Effemi-
nate and indecisive men are scary. They make me feel frightened and
unsafe. Masculinity entails strength, courage, confidence and deci-
siveness, and a masculine man puts these traits into action. These are
noble traits and should not be destroyed.

Early on in our marriage, I noticed that when I went to my husband with a problem, his first reaction was to try to come up with a
solution. This did not upset me as, apparently, it does some women
who think the man should simply listen to her and reassure her with
sympathy and understanding. I want more than just his sympathy

and understanding. I also want a solution! And it is comforting to me to know that he can usually give me one. Furthermore, his act of problem solving *is* treating me with sympathy and understanding. He does understand that I am upset, and his emotional support for me is demonstrated by the fact that he tries to find a solution. I also have learned that there are men who do not like to listen to women repeating their problem for hours on end. (If women want to have that kind of conversation, they need to find other women to talk to.)

Romance

Romance is the recognition and the celebration of the differences between the sexes. Romance is what sparks joy and excitement in the love relationships between men and women. Without the knowledge and acceptance of how men and women are different, there can be no romance.

Romantic love is a special kind of love, a love I reserved for a person of the opposite sex who reflects my deepest values. My romantic love is an emotional response to the virtues and character of my husband. I fell in love with a man who is a reflection of myself. We both look at life the same way and have the same emotional responses to events that affect our values and to art that expresses our values. A romantic relationship is exclusive. My husband and I share with each other our inner, most important private thoughts, fears, joys and so on. We focus on each other; the happiness of both is important to both.

A romantic relationship cannot be between two "best friends." It may start out that way, but once romance begins, the relationship takes on a different meaning. A romantic relationship is higher and more special than a friendship. My husband and I are not pals. Friends are equals, but my husband and I are not equals in romance. I look up to him, admire him for his strength, rely on it, and am excited by it, whereas he loves me but does not "look up" to me.

I want my man to be in charge. "In charge" in a romantic relationship doesn't mean he imposes himself on me. It means he uses
his strength and courage to keep me safe, and I want to be able to
rely on that strength and courage; but, as stated earlier, the strength
does not just entail physical strength, but also intellectual and emotional strength. His strength helps to keep me calm when I am feeling
frightened or anxious. I can rely on him to kill the deadly snake or
check out the noise in the middle of the night.

My desire to have the man in charge does not in any way imply
that I blindly follow him. My man has to meet my standards. He
must have certain qualities such as strength, confidence, rationality,
intelligence, and so on. If my judgment were regularly better than
the man's, I would not be attracted to him. His judgment doesn't always have to be better than mine, however; I evaluate his decisions,
and may disagree and point out when he is wrong, but when he is
right I expect and want him to take action. I want to feel as though
he is a man who knows what to do. This isn't to say that he can't
make mistakes or that he has to decide on something right away, but
it matters to me that he has the confidence to take action when he
does decide. I want him to be decisive—that makes me feel safe.
When I trust and respect the man's judgment, I can relax and bask
in the security that he provides and support him in the action he
takes.

There is another difference between men and women that needs
to be understood in order for romance to flourish: the man needs to
set the romantic tone. The reason for this is that women need to be
in the mood for sex. On a day-to-day basis, I pursue values and goals
just as men do. With sex, my husband is still pursuing a value—me.
He is pursuing me just as he pursues the rest of his values, and I become the object of his pursuit. I become the value that he is pursuing.
So, in the area of sex, I have to shift my thinking from being a pursuer
of values to being pursued. That is why romance is so important to
me, because in romance I shift emotionally, and special events like

candlelit dinners get me in the mood. When a man gives me flowers, it reminds me that I am different, that he recognizes it and likes it. And I melt.

The relationship can be jeopardized, however, if a man shares his romantic feelings with a woman too soon. When I was dating, if a man expressed love for me too early, I concluded that he didn't know enough about me to evaluate me, so how can he love me? I thought that it wasn't me that he loved; it was anyone. He must be needy. That was a big negative. Or I thought that I was being manipulated. Another negative. When serious emotions such as love are expressed later in the relationship, it means more when it is finally said. Saying "I love you" isn't to be taken lightly. Waiting to hear the real words with meaning has a big impact, as it should.

Due to the physical and resulting psychological differences between the sexes, my romantic love for my husband is the most intense and rewarding of all my human relationships. It is from this relationship that I fully experience myself as a woman. I also gain an intimate view of life from the perspective of the opposite sex and have concluded that life cannot be fully experienced without a unifying relationship with the opposite sex.

Sex

The ultimate love that my husband and I have for each other is expressed through sex. Sex is the intellectual, emotional, and physical expression of our romantic love. Sex unifies our souls in mind, body and spirit and is the highest tribute that we can give to another. Sex is the physical expression of the intimacy that we share together in spirit. In addition to being an expression of love, sex is also an expression of a sacred commitment to each other. Just as our relationship is personal and private and not to be splattered all over the universe, so is our sex life personal and private. It is not to be shared with anyone else.

For my husband and me to stand naked in body and spirit with each other demands self-confidence. It takes true courage to reveal your innermost self and then reveal yourself in intimacy that involves sexual intercourse. It also takes courage to face someone with one's soul, and prepare to judge and be judged.

In the act of sex, the man plays the leading role. He pursues the woman, initiates sex, and is dominant in the sex act. As a woman, I fully enjoy responding to the man's role. I want to be pursued, to be conquered, and dominated. I want to be his reward for the qualities that I value in him. Sex is a physical reward and it is also a psychological reward. The sex act allows me to experience fully my femininity in contrast to my husband and he can experience his masculinity in contrast to me. Without the integration of our spirits, sex would simply be a physical act without meaning and without reward.

The Magnitude of Sex

Sex is the highest expression of love that you can give to your romantic partner. I have always thought that it is a form of intimacy, a sacred moment that needs to be expressed only with someone that I love passionately.

Although trust is very important to both partners, it is particularly important for me. The sexual act can initially be frightening, because the man has more physical strength: he could potentially harm me, albeit innocently. When I have sex, it is my body that is entered. There are all kinds of thoughts and feelings that go along with that. I must love him enough to allow that to happen, and my resulting feeling is that of submission. Other women have told me that when a man doesn't understand the seriousness of the sex act, it leaves them feeling used, lonely, and sad.

As an individual, I went through a process in order to develop myself. I developed myself alone, and because I developed myself alone, I feel comfortable alone as I am secure in my own thoughts. Once I matured, I sought someone with whom to share my soul. I wanted someone who reflects my deepest values and sees life the same way I do. I wanted to be seen as an individual, and therefore it takes another individual to reflect me and make me feel visible. I want to feel valued and that my value as a person is understood so much so that my life is crucial to my loved one's happiness. This is why I take sex seriously, not casually.

The possibility of a child is another reason why sex is a very serious issue. My actions and that of my partner have the potential to affect someone else, and therefore the issue of sex becomes bigger than just the two of us. People have argued that pregnancy precautions can be taken, or an abortion can be performed, but the precautions don't always work and abortions aren't always an option. Sex can result in a baby. The possibility of pregnancy, and what would be done if that happens, should have already been discussed and agreed upon ahead of time. (Ideally, a child should not come into the picture outside of marriage. Although marriage may not be a requirement for a sexual relationship, marriage certainly simplifies and removes questions about responsibility should a child be the result.)

Romantic / Respectful Gestures

Men making small protective gestures for women such as opening doors or walking on the outside of the sidewalk are acts of kindness. A protective gesture is not a statement about my weakness, it is a statement of his strength and that he is using it to make life easier for me. It is a reminder that I am different from him and, hence, it is a romantic gesture. Plus, some doors are heavy and it actually makes it easier for me to have the help, just as when my husband sees me struggle to open a jar and comes over to save the day. It is compassionate to watch out for people that you care about.

I appreciate those small romantic gestures, which show he cares for me, and I love to be reminded of his strength. Those small gestures keep romance alive. It is Western man that values women, and treats them with high regard. The Western man treats a woman like a queen. When I was growing up, men stood up when a woman entered the room. This was a sign of respect. This demonstration of respect is miles above the uncivilized men of the past who treated women as less than human.

Chivalry

I can take care of myself, but what do I want in my relationship with a man? Do I want a man who worships me and kneels at my feet to propose marriage? Do I want a knight in shining armor to come riding on his horse to rescue me from an uncivilized barbarian? Do I want a man to take off his coat to wrap around me when I am cold? Do I want a man to bring me flowers? Yes. Deep down, I swoon at these thoughts, and I think that all feminine women feel the same way. The desire for chivalry and romance is not dead. I want a man who loves and wants me desperately. Conversely, I want a man worthy of my desire; I want to worship him, and do loving things for him in return. I do need a man, not for my self-worth because I already have self-worth, but I do need him for my romantic happiness.

Marriage and Family

My husband and I both view marriage as an important institution. We view marriage as our public declaration of our exclusive romantic love for each other and our promise to remain faithful to each other. Some people chose to live together without getting married, but we think that marriage seals our commitment to each other. Without a permanent commitment, there is always the risk of separation should the relationship encounter a rough spot. The unspoken message that looms over the relationship is, "I want a way out in case this doesn't work." Of course, marriage is also a risk. It could end in divorce should problems arise that are unresolvable. But the marriage commitment says, "I love you enough to take that risk. I love you enough to raise children with you, face the problems in life with you, and share the joys of life with you."

Sometime after my husband and I married, we had children. There is something intensely romantic about having children. A child is a life that is a result of the love of the parents whether through childbirth or adoption. It bonded us even closer together, and our commitment to each other carried over to our commitment to our children. Our children were a constant reminder of our love for each other as they were growing up, and is still a reminder of it now as we interact with them as adults.

Our family provided a peaceful haven for all of us to flourish as individuals and receive support and/or feedback for our accomplishments, goals, and problems. My husband and I took responsibility for raising our children, teaching them moral behavior, how to make good choices, and how to think. We also tried to instill good values in our children. We strove to make our family a safe, loving place for our children to learn how to make good choices, and learn how to correct their mistakes as they grew up. Just as a proper school helps a child develop his thinking abilities so that he can become an independent individual, so did we as parents. Because the family is where the individual child is valued and developed, and the child eventually grows up to become a citizen, the family is the foundation to the success of the culture as a whole.

The child's upbringing is highly influential in how the child turns out as an adult, and ideally the child needs both parents to guide him as he grows up. Children learn about the nature of each sex. They learn from their fathers what it means to be a man, learn from their mothers about womanhood, and learn in what respects both sexes are the same. It is during childhood that the child forms his basic methods of cognition, and my husband and I took responsibility for providing an environment that facilitated this development. We each gave our children different experiences from which they gained knowledge. They worked with their dad on activities such as wood working or car maintenance; and with me on cooking or sewing. Each parent may approach the child differently to help with life's challenges. For example, when our children felt sad and discouraged, I tended to comfort them, whereas my husband tended to give them encouragement. The relationship that develops between a child and his parents is unique and cannot be replaced.

Marriage is the ideal institution for raising children. According to the Center for Law and Social Policy (Parke 2003), children who are raised by married parents do better than those whose parents are divorced, cohabitating or single. A study by the Centers for Disease Control (2010, 27) concluded,

> children living in nuclear families—that is, in families consisting of two married adults who are the biological or adoptive parents of all children in the family—were generally healthier, more likely to have access to healthcare, and less likely to have definite or severe emotional or behavioral difficulties than children living in nonnuclear families.

Also, in the event of a divorce, separation, or abandonment, the state protects the children, and reconciles any disputes between the husband and wife about parental and property rights.

Sometimes a woman or a man can't find someone to marry, or perhaps have decided against marriage, but want to raise a child. This isn't ideal for the child, but this doesn't necessarily mean that the child will suffer. Single parents can be great parents, and it is better the child be raised in a loving home rather than in an orphanage. But the parent needs to be aware of the possible problems (abandonment issues, lack of an opposite sex parent for a role model, etc.) that can pop up for the child so that the parent is prepared to help him. A child is a human being and his life and upbringing needs to be taken seriously. The decision of whether to raise a child and how to raise him must encompass what is best for him, not just the desires of the parents.

A purpose of the family is to help the child develop his individuality, but the family is not more important than the individual child. If a child grows up and his values clash with those of his parents in a way that cannot be tolerated—the parent is immoral, or conversely, the child has chosen to follow an immoral path—they may choose to disassociate in some way. The child does not owe allegiance, no matter what, to his family—just as the parents do not owe it to their child when he becomes an adult. However, if the parents continue to have a good relationship with their adult children, the family is immensely enjoyable.

Not everyone chooses to marry or to have a family, but that does not change the fact that marriage and family are valid institutions in Western Culture. During the early stages of human evolution, everyone belonged to the community, and property was owned and shared collectively. With the creation of wealth and private property, people wanted to be able to pass it on to their children. In the community, there was no limitation to sexual access, so the correct heirs were difficult to ascertain. With families there was no question as to who the heirs were. Today the family has evolved to mean a whole lot more than just passing on inheritance. People now pursue their happiness by trying to find someone to love and with whom they can create a happy family. Close human relationships are one of life's greatest joys, an immensely important value, and marriage and family can secure and complete that value.

All families are different, just as all marriages are different. Some are good, some bad, and some in between. But the bad marriages or bad families don't mean those institutions as such are not worth pursuing. Healthy people don't get married with the intention to make a bad marriage, nor do responsible people start a family with bad intentions. Most people want to be happy and they want their close relationships to work out.

My husband and I fell in love, married, created a family, and built a life together. With one another we faced all the challenges of raising our children, while experiencing all the joys they brought to us and still bring to us. I wouldn't have it any other way.

References

Centers for Disease Control (2010), "Family Structure and Children's Health in the United States: Findings From the National Health Interview Survey, 2001–2007", *Vital and Health Statistics* 10 (246). Accessed on December 12, 2020 at https://www.cdc.gov/nchs/data/series/sr_10/sr10_246.pdf.

Parke, Mary (2003), "Are Married Parents Really Better for Children?", *Center for Law and Social Policy*. Accessed on December 12, 2020 at https://www.clasp.org/sites/default/files/public/resources-and-publications/states/0086.pdf.

Rand, Ayn (1968), "An Answer to Readers (About a Woman President)," *The Objectivist* 7 (12): 1–3.

APPENDIX 5: BY JEFFREY PERREN

MASCULINITY AND FEMININITY, AS EXEMPLIFIED IN THE FILM *THE BIG COUNTRY*

(This essay contains film spoilers.)

Many readers are likely to be familiar with *The Big Country*, starring Gregory Peck and Jean Simmons. In the 1958 film, an eastern sea captain travels to Texas to wed the daughter of a mammoth-ranch owner. While the movie is often discussed as both an outstanding example of the western genre and as part of the mythos of the American hero, here we'll focus on the work as depicting a few distinct and varying concepts of masculinity and femininity.

Sea captain Jim McKay (Gregory Peck) arrives in Texas on the stage in well-to-do Eastern dress, complete with derby hat. He's instantly tagged as "a dude" by the locals, including several members of the hated Hannassey clan. Leading the way is oldest-son Buck (Chuck Connors), a swinish brute who favors drinking and whoring. The family is headed by putative ruffian Rufus (Burl Ives), who is locked in a perpetual feud with the wealthy Major Henry Terrill (Charles Bickford). Major Terrill also happens to be the father of McKay's fiancee, Pat Terrill (Carroll Baker).

When Pat rides McKay from the stage in town to the Terrill ranch, the Hannassey boys intercept them. Buck grabs McKay's derby hat and throws it in the air, and all the boys shoot at it. McKay maintains his good humor, but Pat is indignant. She grabs a rifle and points it at Buck. McKay disarms Pat to defuse the situation, but then the boys rope McKay like a calf and have their fun pulling him this way and that. Finally, they cut him loose, Buck impugns McKay's manhood, and the boys ride off.

So far we have a fairly standard western saga scenario. But in the hands of director William Wyler and screenwriter James Webb (adapting from the novelette by Donald Hamilton) we can look forward to a unique story superbly painted on an epic-sized canvas. An important part of that uniqueness is the colliding views of what it is to be a man or a woman.

Angrily discussing the hazing of McKay by Buck, Major Terrill suggests that McKay's "gentlemanly forbearance" is misplaced in this semi-wild country. McKay tries to explain why he didn't think the incident serious enough to justify Pat's gunplay. The film's early exposition of Terrill's and McKay's perspectives suggests already conflicting ideas of what constitutes a masculine man, dramatic conflicts that will only heighten as the movie unreels.

Another example soon occurs. Terrill's foreman, Steve Leech (Charlton Heston), slyly tries to coax McKay to ride "Old Thunder," a horse who reveals at once his habitual temper. Quickly catching on to the joke, McKay spurns the invitation—but at the cost of furthering the opinion by onlookers that he's unmanly for refusing. The audience clearly knows otherwise, but—with this action coupled with McKay's demurring to take revenge for the buggy ride hazing—even McKay's fiancee is beginning to wonder.

To contrast Pat's vain, emotionalist view of masculinity, we're introduced to her schoolteacher friend Julie Maragon (Jean Simmons). We see at once in her a wiser and much more emotionally mature woman—one who will later say of the hero, "Jim McKay is clearly afraid of only one thing: that someone will accuse him of being a showoff."

This provides a further contrasting view of proper masculinity: the violent-action orientation of Terrill, Leech, et al. versus the prudential reasoning of McKay (echoed by Julie).

Yet far from being the stereotypical man of intellect with no physical skills who fears strenuous action, McKay proves he's fully up to any task. He describes his past as a sea captain ("I was keelhauled the first time I crossed the equator"). And, privately, he arranges with the honorable Mexican ranch hand Ramon to secretly ride Old Thunder—and does until, despite being thrown multiple times and unlike anyone before him, he finally subdues the formerly unbroken stallion.

McKay inadvertently amplifies the prevailing views of his character when he sets off alone to scout the area, ostensibly to buy a wedding present for Pat—in the form of the ranch formerly owned by Julie's grandfather, a once-prosperous ranch called The Big Muddy.

As in many westerns, this all-important section of well-watered land will form the basis for the major plot events to come. But here it performs an equally important role: giving Jim and Julie a chance to know one another better, to better show us their characters.

The scenes between them manifest how his sense of humor and easy-going confidence closely match hers. Even more germane, it amplifies how, in contrast to the rash behavior of Rufus Hannassey and Major Terrill, McKay approaches conflicts more thoughtfully and humanely. He believes if he buys Big Muddy from Julie he can keep the peace between both clans, as her grandfather had for years.

Tragically but not surprisingly, the message McKay left with Ramon to pass to Major Terrill (that the experienced sea captain knew well how to navigate this new land) was never delivered. Terrill sends Leech out with several ranch hands to locate "the lost fiance" and to return him safely.

The crew is unable to find him after a day and night of searching, but then McKay stumbles onto Leech's campfire-illuminated camp and casually asks for a cup of coffee. Leech angrily orders word sent back to Major Terrill—then even more angrily confronts McKay for wandering off in a strange land, forcing him and his men to search for hours on end. McKay reacts placidly to the anger, saying that he was never lost. "I knew exactly where I was at every moment." In yet another example of his masculine confidence, his first-handed understanding of his self, McKay doesn't even object when Leech calls him a liar.

Soon after, back at the ranch, the foreman offers to settle the argument with a fist fight. We instantly have another illustration of McKay's stoic masculinity when he says outright, "You're gambling, Leech. You're gambling that if we fight you'll win. You're gambling that if you win Miss Terrill will admire you for it."

But Leech isn't an entirely black villain; he demonstrates an element of his own virtuous manliness when he declares: "Out here we keep a lady's name out of an argument." All present disperse after it becomes evident that Jim will continue to refuse to fight.

Leech is merely disappointed, but Pat is devastated. This is the last straw. She threatens to call off the engagement. Back in the house, she shouts: "Don't you care what other people think?!" He tells her, "I'm not responsible for what other people think. Only for what I am."

In McKay's worldview moral independence is a core feature of masculinity. He then says he'll move into town in the morning, adding, "I think we both need time to think this over."

Considered reasoning is another masculine feature. The film shows us again how—for McKay, for a moral man—thought and action are integrated.

Later that same night, McKay knocks on Leech's door and makes clear he's ready to fight, but with the understanding that it'll be known only between the two of them. Leech immediately jumps to the conclusion, "I can understand you wouldn't want anyone to know."

The audience understands, however, that the intimation that McKay is cowardly—and wants to avoid potentially being embarrassed by having it known he was beaten—is clearly bunk. But that very variation in moral evaluations of the same events is exactly what helps the audience see the differences in Leech's view of manhood versus McKay's.

McKay is a self-contained man, ethically. He needs no one's approval beyond his own in order to support his self-esteem, while welcoming that of any similarly first-handed person (such as Julie) whose standards he shares.

Like Major Terrill, Leech is more the traditionalist in many respects—inclined to see masculinity in terms of physical courage and ability, ready with his fists, brave but largely unthinking. (Buck Hannassey is an even more pronounced, and devoid of compensating virtue, exemplar of this archetype.) By sharp contrast, McKay is more Randian in nature. He has physical courage but also moral backbone, fortitude resting on a foundation of reason and independence.

After the long and brutally punishing fight to a standstill, McKay asks Leech, "Now tell me, Leech. What did we prove?" A simple question, but brilliantly revealing how pointless is physical conflict divorced from a proper purpose, in McKay's philosophy.

Pat is unaware of this event, later complaining to Julie about Jim's unwillingness to "stand up for his honor," as she might put it. Here she evinces how she's much more aligned with Leech or her father in her own perspective on masculinity (though we've had plenty of strong hints of this earlier). But Julie upbraids her, saying: "How many times does a man have to win you?"

In other ways Julie shows she has her own, feminine version of McKay's courage and independence of spirit along with an equal amount of moral clarity and staunchness, which she exhibits again later in the film. Buck Hannassey convinces his father Rufus that Julie is "sweet on" Buck. Rufus then orders Buck to bring Julie to the family ranch to arrange the marriage, whereby Rufus can acquire The Big Muddy. Buck then kidnaps Julie and brings her to Rufus, who soon realizes that Buck has been lying. But Rufus coerces Julie to sign over the deed anyway. Having already sold the property to McKay, she does so without resistance.

Rufus, rough but no dummy, immediately sniffs that something is afoul, and he confronts her with his suspicion. She replies, "I sold it to the one man no one can ride roughshod over. I sold it to Jim McKay."

Nevertheless, Rufus keeps Julie captive, knowing Terrill will try to rescue her and provide him an opportunity to kill his rival. During the night, Buck forces open the door to her bedroom and his behavior makes clear he intends to rape her. After an intense struggle, Rufus enters and stops him, swearing he "may have to kill you [Buck] someday."

Here we see that even Rufus has his own idea of proper manhood. Coarse though he is, the Hannassey clan leader is enough of a "southern gentleman" to disdain taking a woman by force. "For once, try to be the man I raised you to be," he declares to Buck at one point. It's clear that, despite their similarities, there are still important differences in how father and son exemplify masculinity.

Soon after, Major Terrill, Leech, and their men arrive at Blanco Canyon, a narrow but deep gorge outside the entrance to the Hannassey ranch. McKay learns of this and rides out to them, ostensibly to stop the war but actually to rescue Julie.

Once Jim arrives, Julie tries to defend him from Buck (who has threatened to kill McKay if she gives away the game), demonstrating her own feminine form of bravery as well as her love for Jim. Rufus quickly catches on to the shared feelings of the pair and exhorts Buck to look: "Can't you see?!"

Jim and Julie, for the first time fully aware of it themselves, seal their romantic understanding with an exchanged long look.

Rufus once again purveys his notion of manliness when he proposes that—rather than a six-gun battle or fist fight—Buck and McKay compete with the dueling pistols Jim has in his saddlebags. "Have you got the stomach for a real fight, gentleman style!?" Rufus barks at Buck.

They duel; McKay is slightly wounded when Buck cheats, firing ahead of the signal. McKay stares down Buck and prepares to return fire. Buck reveals his actual lack of virility when, at the prospect of standing up to McKay's single shot, the brute cowers behind a water tank. McKay fires into the dirt and contemptuously tosses away the gun, showing us another aspect of his *genuine* manliness: nobility. He refuses to kill so unworthy an opponent when his own life is no longer at risk.

As the film's end draws near, Terrill gathers his men and orders all to advance into the canyon to battle the Hannasseys. Finally, Leech rebels. The certain slaughter of his crew, along with the dawning realization of the noble character of Jim McKay, are having their effect. The Major sets off on his own. But a moment later, Leech reluctantly follows, his loyalty outweighing his other moral concerns. In The Big Country, even when the characters are mistaken they exhibit a rare patrician stature.

Fortunately, McKay is able to get Julie safely away from the Hannassey property, though not yet out of the canyon, and avoid the massacre about to come. Once that battle is complete, McKay and Julie ride out—exchanging yet another knowing look. That fixed gaze conveys to the audience that this perfectly masculine man and feminine woman are about to embark on a lifetime of inseparable, admiring devotedness, a type of life possible only atop a bedrock of rationality and self-reliance.

* * *

Addendum from Ronald Pisaturo

In the above essay, Jeffrey Perren contrasts two conceptions of masculinity depicted in *The Big Country*. In the following addendum, I will contrast the movie's depiction of masculinity on the one hand and femininity on the other.

Pat and Julie are both beautiful, strong-willed, well-spoken, and adept at handling a rifle. The difference between them is their judgment of McKay. In the film, it is the men who drive the action. The role of the women is to judge the men.

Recall this passage from Chapter 2:

> The essence of masculinity is rational, decisive, indomitable leadership. The essence of femininity is the passion to judge individual men, and to find one man that lives up to the woman's highest standards.

Julie inherited The Big Muddy from her grandfather. Under her ownership, the property has fallen into disrepair. Indeed, while walking on the front porch, McKay falls through the deteriorated floorboards. There are no cattle to be seen. But we do not fault Julie for this state of decay. The presumption is that a woman is not physically capable of maintaining such a property. If, on the other hand, a property owned by McKay—or any man—were in such condition, we would form a low opinion of the man.

Julie is far superior to Buck intellectually. Nevertheless, she must be rescued from Buck twice—by a man, first Rufus and then McKay.

In the second rescue, when McKay arrives on the scene, Julie's role is simply to convey—surreptitiously or inadvertently—information to McKay. This information is useless in Julie's mind alone. But once McKay infers the information, he puts it to use by means of his masculine power. He acts decisively and swiftly to overpower Buck.

Despite his modesty, McKay does tame Old Thunder, demonstrating his masculine power to tame nature—a power he will need to run The Big Muddy. He does fight Leech, demonstrating his masculine power to fight men—a power he will need to outfight Buck and save the woman he loves.

Imagine the movie with the sex of each character reversed. Such a movie would be ludicrous, with none of the characters worthy of romance.

As Jim and Julie ride out of Blanco Canyon in triumph, with the final background music playing, their riding path twice narrows so that they must ride in single file. Both times, Jim rides out front, with Julie right behind. Recall this passage from Chapter 2:

> No matter how technologically advanced a society becomes, so long as human beings remain physical beings, there will always be new adventures that have a significant physical element requiring physical prowess; and so long as the current physical differences between men and women persist, it will always be man who is most able to lead the way in facing those challenges.

REFERENCES

Aetna (2021), "Gender Affirming Surgery", *Medical Clinical Policy Bulletins*, Number 0615. Accessed on January 21, 2021 at http://www.aetna.com/cpb/medical/data/600_699/0615.html.

Altman, Dennis (1971), *Homosexual Oppression and Liberation.* New York: Avon Books.

——— (1982), *The Homosexualization of America: The Americanization of The Homosexual.* New York: St. Martin's Press.

American Psychiatric Association (1973), "Homosexuality: Proposed Change in DSM-II". Arlington, VA: Author.

American Psychological Association. (2008), "Answers to your questions: For a better understanding of sexual orientation and homosexuality." Washington, DC: Author. Accessed on May 4, 2013 at www.apa.org/topics/sorientation.pdf.

American Psychological Association Task Force on Appropriate Therapeutic Responses to Sexual Orientation. (2009), *Report of the Task Force on Appropriate Therapeutic Responses to Sexual Orientation.* Washington, DC: Author.

Anderson, Ryan T. (2015). *Truth Overruled: The Future of Marriage and Religious Freedom.* Washington: Regnery Publishing.

——— (2019), *When Harry Became Sally: Responding to the Transgender Moment.* New York: Encounter Books.

Anthem (2021), "Gender Reassignment Surgery", *Clinical UM Guideline*, # CG-SURG-27. Accessed on March 21, 2021 at https://www.anthem.com/dam/medpolicies/abcbs/active/guidelines/gl_pw_a051166.html.

Aristotle (1941), *Poetics*. Translation by Ingram Bywater. In *The Basic Works of Aristotle*. Edited by Richard McKeon. New York: Random House.

——— (2000), *Metaphysics*. Translation by W.D. Ross. The Internet Classics Archive by Daniel C. Stevenson, Web Atomics. Accessed on July 21, 2000 at http://classics.mit.edu//Aristotle/metaphysics.html.

Bailey, J. M. (2003), "Biological Perspectives on Sexual Orientation", *Psychological Perspectives on Lesbian, Gay, and Bisexual Experiences*. Edited by Linda D. Garnets & Douglas C. Kimmel New York: Columbia University Press.

Berger, Peter L. and Thomas Luckmann (1966), *The Social Construction of Reality*. London: Penguin Books.

Bieber, Irving (1987), "On Arriving at the American Psychiatric Association Decision on Homosexuality", *Scientific Controversies*. Edited by H. Tristam Engelhardt Jr and Arthur L. Caplan. Cambridge: Cambridge University Press 417–436.

Bieber, Irving and Toby B. Bieber, Harvey J. Dain, Paul R. Dince, Martin G. Drellich, Henry G. Grand, Ralph H. Gundlach, Malvina W. Kremer, Alfred H. Rifkin, Cornelia B. Wilbur ([1962] 1988), *Homosexuality: A Psychoanalytic Study*. Northvale, New Jersey: Jason Aronson Inc.

Binswanger, Harry (1986), *The Ayn Rand Lexicon*. New York:

Meridian.

California Department of Insurance (n.d), "Consumers: HIV/AIDS." Accessed on June 23, 2013 at http://www.insurance.ca.gov/0100-consumers/0060-information-guides/0050-health/hiv-aids.cfm.

Chall, Leo P. (1961), "A Survey of Advances in Modern Sex Research", *The Encyclopedia of Sexual Behavior.* Edited by Albert Ellis and Albert Abarbanel. New York: Hawthorn Books, 25–34.

Cigna (2021), "Treatment of Gender Dysphoria", *Medical Coverage Policy*, Number 0266. Accessed on March 21, 2021 at https://static.cigna.com/assets/chcp/pdf/coveragePolicies/medical/mm_0266_coveragepositioncriteria_gender_reassignment_surgery.pdf.

Connell, R. W. (1987), *Gender and Power: Society, The Person, and Sexual Politics.* Stanford, California: Stanford University Press.

——— (1992), "A Very Straight Gay: Masculinity, Homosexual Experience, and the Dynamics of Gender", *American Sociological Review* 57: 735–751.

Cory, Donald Webster (1961), "Homosexuality", *The Encyclopedia of Sexual Behavior.* Edited by Albert Ellis and Albert Abarbanel. New York: Hawthorn Books, 485–493.

D'Emilio, John (1993), "Gay Politics and Community in San Francisco", *Psychological Perspectives on Lesbian & Gay Male Experiences.* Second Edition. Edited by Linda D. Garnets & Douglass C. Kimmel. New York: Columbia University Press.

——— ([1983] 1999), "Capitalism and Gay Identity", *The Columbia*

Reader on Lesbians and Gay Men in Media, Society, and Politics. Edited by Larry P. Gross, James D. Woods. New York, Columbia University Press, 48–55. The essay, without the quoted preface, is reprinted from *Powers of Desire: The Politics of Sexuality.* Edited by Ann Snitow, Christine Stansell, & Sharan Thompson. New Feminist Library Series. New York: Monthly Review Press.

Diamond, Lisa M. and Clifford J. Rosky (2016), "Scrutinizing Immutability: Research on Sexual Orientation and U.S. Legal Advocacy for Sexual Minorities," *The Journal of Sex Research,* 53: 4–5, 363–391.

Evans, Susan and Marcus Evans (2021), "First, Do No Harm: A New Model for Treating Trans-Identified Children", *Quillette,* 4 February. Accessed on February 15, 2021 at https://quillette.com/2021/02/04/first-do-no-harm-a-new-model-for-treating-trans-identified-children/.

Foucault, Michel (1978), *The History of Sexuality, Volume I: An Introduction.* Translated from the French by Robert Hurley. New York: Pantheon Books.

——— ([2008] 2010). *The Government of Self and Others. Lectures at the Collège de France, 1982- 1983.* Translated by Graham Burchell. Houndmills and New York: Palgrave Macmillan. Quotation accessed on July 19, 2013 at http://www.michel-foucault.com/quote/2010q.html.

Frontline (n.d.), "Homophobia Questionnaire", *Public Broadcasting System.* Accessed on June 23, 2013 at http://www.pbs.org/wgbh/pages/frontline/shows/assault/etc/quiz.html.

Frumkin, Robert M. (1961) "Sexual Freedom", *The Encyclopedia of*

Sexual Behavior. Edited by Albert Ellis and Albert Abarbanel. New York: Hawthorn Books, 439–449.

Ganna, Andrea *et al.* (2019), "Large-scale GWAS reveals insights into the genetic architecture of same-sex sexual behavior", *Science* 365 (6456), eaat7693.

Garnets, Linda D. & Douglas C. Kimmel (1993), *Psychological Perspectives on Lesbian & Gay Male Experiences.* New York: Columbia University Press.

Garnets and Peplau (2001), "A New Paradigm for Women's Sexual Orientation: Implications for Therapy", *Women & Therapy* 24: 1/2, 111–121.

Gergen, Kenneth J. (1985), "The Social Constructionist Movement in Modern Psychology", *American Psychologist* 40: 266–275.

Gonsiorek, John C. (1991), "The Empirical Basis For The Demise of the Illness Model Of Homosexuality", *Homosexuality: Research Implications for Public Policy.* Edited by John C. Gonsiorek and James D. Weinrich. Newbury Park, CA: Sage Publications, 115–136.

Gonsiorek, John C. and James R. Rudolph (1991), "Homosexual identity: Coming out and other developmental events", *Homosexuality: Research Implications for Public Policy.* Edited by John C. Gonsiorek and James D. Weinrich. Newbury Park, CA: Sage Publications, 161–176.

Halperin, David M. (1990), *One Hundred Years of Homosexuality.* New York: Routledge.

Haslanger, Sally (1993), "On Being Objective and Being Objectified", *A Mind of One's Own: Feminist Essays on Reason and*

Objectivity. Edited by Louise M. Antony and Charlotte Witt. Boulder: Westview Press.

Herek, Gregory M. ([1986] 1993), "On Heterosexual Masculinity: Some Psychical Consequences of the Social Construction of Gender and Sexuality", *American Behavioral Scientist* 29: 563-577. Reprinted in *Psychological Perspectives on Lesbian & Gay Male Experiences*. Edited by Linda D. Garnets and Douglas C. Kimmel. New York: Columbia University Press: 316–330.

——— (1993),"The Context of Anti-Gay Violence; Notes on Cultural and Psychological Heterosexism", *Psychological Perspectives on Lesbian & Gay Male Experiences*. Edited by Linda D. Garnets and Douglas C. Kimmel. New York: Columbia University Press, 89–108.

——— (2000), "Homosexuality", *Encyclopedia of Psychology*. Alan E. Kazdin, Editor-in-Chief. Washington, DC: American Psychological Association and Oxford University Press.

Hicks, Stephen R. C. (2011), *Explaining Postmodernism: Skepticism and Socialism from Rousseau to Foucault* (Expanded Edition). Ockham's Razor Publishing.

Human Rights Campaign. Website accessed on February 27, 2021 at https://www.hrc.org.

Humana (2021), "Gender Reassignment Surgery", *Medical Coverage Policy*, Number HCS-0518-016. Accessed on March 21, 20201 at http://apps.humana.com/tad/Tad_New/Search .aspx?docbegin=G&policyType=medical&searchtype=be-ginswith.

Hume, David ([1777] 1902), *An Enquiry Concerning Human*

Understanding. Edited by L.A. Selby-Bigge. Kindle Edition.

Jones, Stanton L. (2012), "Sexual orientation and reason: On the Implications of False Beliefs About Homosexuality". Accessed on May 27, 2013 at www.christianethics.org.

Kay, Jonathan (2019), "An Interview With Lisa Littman, Who Coined the Term 'Rapid Onset Gender Dysphoria'", *Quillette*, 19 March. Accessed on February 27, 2021 at https://quil-lette.com/2019/03/19/an-interview-with-lisa-littman-who-coined-the-term-rapid-onset-gender-dysphoria/.

LaSala, Michael C. (2011), "Sexual Orientation: Is It Unchangea-ble?", *Psychology Today*. Accessed on July 13, 2013 at http://www.psychologytoday.com/blog/gay-and-lesbian-well-being/201105/sexual-orientation-is-it-unchangeable.

LeVay, Simon (2011), *Gay, Straight and the Reason Why*. New York: Oxford University Press.

Levin, Roy J. and Willy van Berlo (2004), "Sexual Arousal and Or-gasm in Subjects Who Experience Forced or Non-Consensual Sexual Stimulation – A Review", *Journal of Clinical Forensic Medicine 11*: 82–88.

Littman, Lisa (2018), "Parent Reports of Adolescents and Young Adults Perceived to Show Signs of a Rapid Onset of Gender Dysphoria", *PLOS ONE* 13(8): e0202330. Accessed on January 25, 2021 at https://doi.org/10.1371/journal.pone.0202330.

Marcuse, Herbert (1969), "Repressive Tolerance", *A Critique of Pure Tolerance*. Edited by Robert Paul Wolf. Boston: Beacon Press.

Mayer, Lawrence S. and Paul R. McHugh (2016), Sexuality and

Gender: Findings from the Biological, Psychological, and Social Sciences, *The New Atlantis* 50:1–144.

Mazlish, Ed (2013), "Gay Marriage and the Role of State", *Capitalism Magazine*. Accessed on June 2, 2013 at http://capitalismmagazine.com/2013/04/gay-marriage-and-the-role-of-state/.

Parsons, Jeffrey T. and Christian Grov (2012), "Gay Male Identities, Desires, and Sexual Behaviors", *Handbook of Psychology and Sexual Orientation*. Edited by Charlotte J. Patterson and Anthony R. D'Augelli. New York: Oxford University Press, 18–30.

Peikoff, Leonard ([1967] 1990), "The Analytic-Synthetic Dichotomy", *The Objectivist* 6(5)–6(9). Reprinted in *Introduction to Objectivist Epistemology, Expanded Second Edition*. Edited by Harry Binswanger and Leonard Peikoff. New York: Meridian.

——— (1982), *The Ominous Parallels: The End of Freedom in America*. New York: Stein and Day.

——— (1991), *Objectivism: The Philosophy of Ayn Rand*. New York: Dutton.

Peplau, Letitia Anne, Leah R. Spalding, Terri D. Conley, and Rosemary C. Veniegas (1999), "The Development Of Sexual Orientation In Women", *Annual Review of Sex Research* 10: 70–99.

Peplau, Letitia Anne (2001), "Rethinking Women's Sexual Orientation: An Interdisciplinary, Relationship-Focused Approach", *Personal Relationships* 8: 1-19.

——— (2003), "Human Sexuality: How Do Men and Women Differ?", *Current Directions In Psychological Science* 12 (2): 37–40.

Pisaturo, Ronald (2020), A *Validation of Knowledge: A New, Objective Theory of Axioms, Causality, Meaning, Propositions, Mathematics, and Induction*. Norwalk, Connecticut: Prime Mover Press.

Pluckrose, Helen and James A. Lindsay (2020), *Cynical Theories*. Durham, North Carolina: Pitchstone Publishing.

Pullmann, Joy (2019), "6 Crazy School District Responses To Parents Mad About LGBT Indoctrination Of Preschoolers", *The Federalist*, October 18, 2019. Accessed on December 13, 2020 at https://thefederalist.com/2019/10/18/6-crazy-school-district-responses-to-parents-mad-about-lgbt-indoctrination-of-pre-schoolers/.

Rand, Ayn (1957), *Atlas Shrugged*. New York: Random House.

——— ([1964] n.d.), "The Playboy Interview with Philosopher Ayn Rand" *Playboy* 11 (3). Reprinted New Milford, Connecticut: Second Renaissance Books.

——— (1971), "The Psychology of 'Psychologizing'", *The Objectivist* 10 (3): 1–8.

——— (1972), "The Stimulus...", *The Ayn Rand Letter* 1 (8): 1–4.

——— ([1966] 1975), "Philosophy and Sense of Life", *The Objectivist* 5 (2): 1–6. Reprinted in *The Romantic Manifesto*. Second Revised Edition. New York: Signet, 25–33.

——— ([1966–1967] 1990), "Introduction to Objectivist Epistemology", *The Objectivist* 5 (7)–6(2). Reprinted in *Introduction to Objectivist Epistemology*, Expanded Second Edition. Edited by Harry Binswanger and Leonard Peikoff. New York: Meridian.

———— ([1968] 1990), "Of Living Death" (Part 1), *The Objectivist* 7 (9): 1–6. Reprinted in *The Voice of Reason*, New York: Meridian, 46–63.

Ratner, Ellen F. (1993), "Treatment Issues for Chemically Dependent Lesbians and gay Men", *Psychological Perspectives on Lesbian & Gay Male Experiences*, 567–578.

Rostand, Edmond ([1898] [1923] 1980), *Cyrano de Bergerac*. Translated into English verse by Brian Hooker. Toronto: Bantam Books.

Sawyer, Diane (2015), "Bruce Jenner The Interview", *20/20*, 24 April. ABC News. Partial transcript published by *Us Weekly*, accessed on March 28, 2021 at https://www.usmagazine.com/entertainment/news/bruce-jenner-interview-with-diane-sawyer-read-us-weeklys-live-blog-2015244/.

Schwartz, Peter (1999), "Gender Tribalism", *Return of the Primitive*. New Expanded Edition of *The New Left: The Anti-Industrial Revolution* by Ayn Rand. Edited by Peter Schwartz. New York: Meridian, 205–216.

Shrier, Abigail (2020), *Irreversible Damage: The Transgender Craze Seducing Our Daughters*. Washington: Regnery Publishing.

Socarides, Charles W. (1992), "Sexual Politics And Scientific Logic: The Issue Of Homosexuality", *The Journal of Psychohistory*, 19(3). Transcription accessed June 23, 2013 at http://www.kidhistory.org/homopolo.html.

Spiegel, Alix (2002), "81 Words", *This American Life*. Transcript of radio broadcast. Accessed June 3, 2013 at http://www.thisamericanlife.org/radio-archives/episode/204/transcript.

Steyn, Mark (2013), "Tiptoeing on Ever-Thinner Eggshells", *Orange County Register* April 5, 2013.

Thompson, C. Bradley (2012), "The New Abolitionism: Why Education Emancipation is the Moral Imperative of our Time", *The Objective Standard*, 7(4): 13–37.

Walsh, George (1970), "Herbert Marcuse, Philosopher of the New Left", *The Objectivist* 9 (9): 7–16, 9 (10): 8–16, 9 (11): 8–16, 9 (12): 6–13.

Weinberg, George (1972), *Society and the Homosexual*. New York: St Martin's Press.

——— (2012), "Homophobia: Don't Ban the Word — Put It in the Index of Mental Disorders", *The Huffington Post*. Accessed on July 11, 2013 at http://www.huffingtonpost.com/george-weinberg/homophobia-dont-ban-the-w_b_2253328.html.

Wolf, Sherry (2004), "The Roots of Gay Oppression", *International Socialist Review* 37. Accessed on June 15, 2013 at http://isreview.org/issues/37/gay_oppression.shtml.

——— (2009), *Sexuality and Socialism*. Chicago: Haymarket Books.

INDEX OF PERSONS AND ORGANIZATIONS

ABOUT THE AUTHORS

Ronald Pisaturo was a founder and President of American Renaissance School, a private high school with high academic standards. The school, located in White Plains, New York, operated in the 1980s. Mr. Pisaturo is also the author of *A Validation of Knowledge: A New, Objective Theory of Axioms, Causality, Meaning, Propositions, Mathematics, and Induction, The Longevity Argument,* and *The Merchant of Mars.* Articles by Mr. Pisaturo have appeared in *Philosophy of Science, The Imaginative Conservative, The Federalist, Quillette, The Intellectual Activist, Barron's, Capitalism Magazine,* many newspapers, and his personal Web site at www.ronpisaturo.com. Plays by Mr. Pisaturo that have been produced include *Escape From Eden* and *Brothers, Not Keepers.*

Charlotte Cushman has AMI and AMS Montessori certifications and more than forty years of teaching experience. She co-owned and operated two Montessori schools, one with her husband. She speaks to the general public on education, has written numerous articles in periodicals such as *The American Thinker,* and has authored three books: *Montessori: Why It Matters for Your Child's Success and Happiness, Effective Discipline the Montessori Way,* and *Your Life Belongs to You.*

Jeffrey Perren is a novelist, the author of *The Hanse Rival* and many others from ClioStory Publishing. His non-fiction work has been published in magazines and on websites from the U.S. to New Zealand, including Breitbart and Pajamas Media. At age 17, he received the Bank of America Fine Arts award. He has viewed, conservatively, over 10,000 films produced before 1970.

www.ingramcontent.com/pod-product-compliance
Lightning Source LLC
LaVergne TN
LVHW051628080426
835511LV00016B/2238